Anonymus

Original thoughts, essays and stanzas

written by the pupils of the San Francisco public schools

Anonymus

Original thoughts, essays and stanzas
written by the pupils of the San Francisco public schools

ISBN/EAN: 9783743328969

Manufactured in Europe, USA, Canada, Australia, Japa

Cover: Foto ©Thomas Meinert / pixelio.de

Manufactured and distributed by brebook publishing software
(www.brebook.com)

Anonymus

Original thoughts, essays and stanzas

ORIGINAL

Thoughts, Essays AND Stanzas

WRITTEN BY THE

PUPILS

OF THE

San Francisco Public Schools

EMBRACING

Names of Writers and the Schools and Grades
to which they belong.

Together with the Cuts of the Writers who are the Winners of the Prizes
offered by the Merchants of San Francisco, and the Engravings
of the Pupils whose Essays and Stanzas deserve Recog-
nition because of their Combined Merit.

" All things I thought I knew,
But now confess, the more I know, I know, I know the less."

ANDREW J. MOULDER.
Superintendent of Public Schools, San Francisco. Cal.

GIRLS' HIGH SCHOOL, COR. SCOTT AND GEARY STREETS.

Introduction.

IN the preparation of this work, it has been the Publishers' aim to present to the Public the Essays and Stanzas of the Pupils of San Francisco's Public Schools, with the strictest accuracy in regard to following the manuscript. To be fair and impartial in the selection of the Essays according to age, grade and school, and to be true and just in the conclusions necessarily drawn from them, it is necessary to bear in mind that they are yet children with unmatured intellect.

While thus striving to be accurate in the selection of these Essays and Stanzas, we do not present to the Public a work where childish error is not to be found, for we have followed as closely as possible the manuscript from the pupil's pen, and in consequence would request the public to overlook any error that may occur, either by the writer or publishers.

When these Essays and Stanzas were submitted to the Merchants, who offered the Prizes for competition, they awarded the Prizes with the best judgment that they possessed, taking into consideration the writing, spelling, composition and general appearance of the Essay. We have avoided favor in all quarters, not offering fulsome adulation on one side nor undue denunciation on the other; but while stipulating that the work contains some of the brightest thoughts of our Public School Pupils, full of sunshine and happiness, and childish extracts from the brains of ambitious scholars.

We contemplate an advancement in the general development and character of the language found in these pages by the manner in which they have devoted intellectual ability and untiring energy in this work.

If then there be found within these covers aught that may seem unlike the childish language that we expect, or aught that may seem harsh to those directly or indirectly interested, do not look upon these pages as from Cooper or Hugo, but bear in mind that from these writers there may develop a Cooper or Hugo for the future.

In writing upon the Industries of San Francisco, it is necessary that the Pupils of our Schools should have constant training upon these different subjects so that they may write more intelligently upon the subject in the future when the occasion presents itself.

In conclusion, we beg to present this work to the Public, asking no favors, but trusting that these Thoughts, Essays and Stanzas will meet with the approval of the reader.

"Expect not the juvenile to write with that intelligence which has taken you a lifetime to learn."

THE PUBLISHERS.

San Francisco, Nov., 1894.

INDEX TO WRITERS.

INDEX TO WRITERS.

ALICE B. CONNELLY.

Carriages.

OW many of us ever pause to think, as we drive along a country road or well-kept city street, in a decidedly comfortable conveyance, of the labor that is expended on or of the wonderful construction of the vehicles of the present day?

Not many. I fancy, for we happy-go-lucky Americans are apt to take too much for granted; to have a thing is all that is necessary, where or how it came is of no moment to us, simply we have it and are satisfied.

However, carriages are something that to the careful observer are extremely interesting. The processes through which the simplest carts have to go before reaching a finished state show how intricate must be their construction.

The manufacture of conveyances gives labor to more men, I imagine, than any other industry—woodmen, miners, foundry-men, tanners, painters and cloth-makers as well as the men who by combining the work of the laborers I have mentioned construct the cart, wagon, carriage or whatever it happens to be. It is not *one* man but *many* men who built the vehicle, for each part is built by a man who is master of the art of construction of that especial part.

To go over the ware-rooms of a fine carriage factory of to-day is like going to an Academy of Fine Arts; for if you do not view beautiful paintings that are masterpieces from some gifted hand, you see many masterpieces, the different parts of which are masterpieces of the mental and mechanical skill of the philosopher who is always designing, scheming and contriving to add some new and important feature to his trade that will enable mankind to have higher and better grades of goods.

Of course, "Fair Science" with her grand advances comes in with easier and better modes of working. The old time forge, used for welding iron, with its flames and smoke, has been done away with to a certain extent, by the wonderful appliance of electricity—that wonder from which the present age receives its name "The Electric Age." The work of welding is carried on with more facility with the aid of this power.

The firm of "Studebaker Bros.," of Indiana, stands as fair an example of carriage manufacture as can be desired. The origin of the firm was extremely obscure. The father, John Studebaker, having employed himself as blacksmith in the town of Ashland, Ohio, here in the little, humble village blacksmith shop the foundation was laid for one of the finest firms in the United States.

The four brothers who constitute the firm have by the constant pursuance of their talents and duty added *much* to carriage industry throughout America, and I may say the world.

The elegant landaus, broughams, victorias, phaetons, surreys, carts, etc., that are yearly manufactured by Studebakers are in every way of such elegance and perfection as to make the observer wonder if there is anything more to be desired in this line of industry.

But who can tell? The next age, with the advantages of science, and the many new perfections that are constantly being added, may produce finer results than those from which we are benefited; but it is doubtful if carriage manufacture be much improved upon.

ALICE B. CONNELLY,
1630 Pierce Street.

Hamilton Grammar School, Graduate Class '94.

The above writer won the prize awarded by Studebaker Bros. Manufacturing Co.

BIOGRAPHY OF ALICE B. CONNELLY.

MISS ALICE BEATRICE CONNELLY, daughter of Francis J. and Alice P. Connelly, a graduate of 1894, was born in San Francisco, California, July 3, 1876. Her paternal ancestors were of vigorous North of Ireland stock, and on the mother's side she is of English descent. Her great-great-grandfather, Lot Hawkins, settled in New Jersey in early Colonial days. Her great-grandfather, Job Hawkins, who while very young served as a drummer boy in Colonel Jonathan Johnson's Regiment of the Connecticut Line of the Continental Army during the Revolutionary struggle, was born at New Milford, Connecticut, and died at the same place, at the advanced age of one hundred years. He was also a soldier of the War of 1812. Inheriting the loyal spirit of this ancestor, and herself "a staunch friend of her country and zealous of her cause," it is not strange that Miss Connelly is about to identify herself with the Society of the Daughters of the American Revolution, a society which aims to keep alive the memory of those who fought and died for their country.

Her early education was directed by her mother, until she entered the public schools of her native town. Her first entrance upon school life was in the Powell Street Primary School under the charge of Mrs. Cordelia Newhall and Mrs. N. R. Craven, Principal ; from thence, on account of change of residence, to the Emerson Primary, with Miss Ida Shaw as instructor.

Alice was a child of marked intelligence, of affectionate and winning manners, and in her home has always been a benediction and a joy. A thorough student, she has fully profited by the advantages offered for her mental growth. Of the specially notable traits of her character is her deep and personal attachment to those with whom she has been brought into special relations, and is one of the secrets of her success as a student and pupil.

She is an enthusiast in music, developing in early childhood a marked talent in that direction ; and under the guidance of Professor Hugo Mansfeldt has devoted much time and earnest study to this subject, with a corresponding degree of success, and through these efforts has become a musician of no common grade. She is also a fine elocutionist.

Although her school life has been frequently interrupted through sickness, thereby lengthening her term of study, yet we find her always diligent, impatient of the delay, and anxious to go forward in the work which she early marked out for herself, which neither sickness or any other adversity could for one moment cause her to swerve from.

In 1889 she entered the Hamilton Grammar School, Wm. A. Robertson, Principal, and with increasing zeal turned her attention to the studies of this more advanced grade with the same spirit of active inquiry that had characterized her earlier efforts. After a three years' course of study, she was May 23, 1894, graduated from Miss Ella J. Morton's class, receiving one of the class medals awarded, her scholarship record ranking among the foremost of the school.

Having completed the grammar school course and mastered the alphabet of her education, she has now entered upon the course of study prescribed by the State Normal School at San Jose, the examination for which she has recently successfully passed, with the view of fitting herself for a teacher. With joyful anticipation she entered September 4th upon this field of labor, where for the present we will leave her.

RÉNÉ E. DUMONTELLE.

SWIMMING.

S WIMMING is an artificial exercise that expands the chest, develops the muscles of the arms, strengthens and fills out the lower limbs. It confers presence of mind and confidence in one's self. It is more of a tonic to swim in salt water than fresh, as the salt has a slightly irritating effect on the skin, which is beneficial.

The late Alexander Mott, of the college of physicians and surgeons of New York, said : '' That a good, vigorous swim in sea water, at the proper season, was of more good to dyspeptic persons than all the medicines of the day.''

When a person learns to swim, he swims first on his breast. He assumes nearly a horizontal position, with his breast prone to the water and the heels near the surface. To effect propulsion, the arms are flexed at the same time and drawn closely to the body ; then they are simultaneously and rapidly extended.

The hands should be kept flat, the fingers closed, the thumb placed by the side of the first finger, and one must reach out as far as possible, for the farther he reaches the faster he will swim ; he then draws the legs well up, while each hand is brought around, one to the right and the other to the left.

He strikes out strongly with his legs. The secret of good swimming is to kick with the legs far apart. Breathing should be unrestrained and without gasping, sputtering or sudden heaving. A safe rule is to take a full breath at every stroke.

Breast swimming is the most common, and the only one possible for long distances ; with a strong, favorable tide in the Thames, one mile has been swam in eleven minutes forty-three seconds.

Swimming on the back is more easily learned than breast swimming, the body being more horizontal.

In diving, the hands are brought together in front to cleave the water and to protect the head ; the legs are kept straight, the heels touching each other.

When a swimmer attempts to rescue a drowning man, the swimmer must approach him from behind and keep him from sinking by placing the hands under the armpits, taking care that the struggler does not seize him, or both might be drowned.

It is easier to swim in salt water than in fresh, as the salt water is heavier than the swimmer and, therefore, can buoy

2

him up. The best time for swimming is between breakfast and luncheon.

Harry Gurr is said to be the inventor of the overhand stroke in 1863, but H. Gardener won the championship in 1862, in Manchester, in using the overhand stroke. The side stroke was introduced by G. Peters in 1850.

Dr. Behrens says: "That foremost among means for the full and harmonious development of all parts and functions of the human body stands swimming, an exercise safely used even by very delicate and debilitated constitutions."

RÉNÉ E. DUMONTELLE,

423 Twenty-sixth Street.

Columbia Grammar School, 8th Grade.

The above writer won the First Prize awarded by the Olympic Salt Water Co.

BIOGRAPHY—RÉNÉ E. DUMONTELLE.

RÉNÉ E. DUMONTELLE, the successful competitor for the first prize on swimming, is a boy of exceptional tact and ability, studious to a degree and thorough in all detail. Being born in the city of San Francisco, California, on the 10th day of May, 1880, he is titled a native son. At a very early age he developed quite a strong desire for learning, for at the age of four years he was attending the Kindergarten School and showed a remarkable ability for a child of that age.

Having graduated from the Columbia Primary to the Columbia Grammar School, Mrs. L. K. Burke, Principal, which he now attends, he has always showed a marked attention to the discipline.

In 1889 he sailed on the good ship Bourgogone, a French vessel, with his mother and sister to visit his grandparents at Senons, France, and for the purpose, at the same time, of visiting the Paris Exposition. While there he gave special attention to every detail that came within his observation, visiting the Exposition on every available opportunity. One can readily imagine the immense value of this experience.

After visiting Senons, he made a trip to Bourgundy, France, where he visited his grandparents on his father's side, making a stay of about two weeks.

After a stay of nearly three months upon the Continent, he,

on the 20th day of July of the same year, embarked on the same vessel and sailed for his native land.

Arriving in New York after a pleasant trip over "old ocean," Réné, preparatory to his departure for California, took in the places of interest in and about the metropolis of America, and stored up in his mind many features that time will never erase.

The subject of this sketch is a violinist of no small importance for his age, having studied under the able Professor T. D. Herzog, 414 Ellis street, of this city. He now wields his bow over the ancient body of a two-hundred-year-old instrument.

Réné is the son of the well-known marble importer and manufacturer, E. Dumontelle, whose works are at 523-525 Fifth Street, of this city.

It is with pleasure and pride that his friends can say that for this student there must be a successful future in store for him, and that he has carried away the gold medal of the Lurline Baths is more than creditable both to himself and his present teacher, Miss Nellie O'Laughlin.

Sunset from Bolinas Ridge.

The warm September afternoon was drawing to a close, when after a wearisome journey of several hours we at length reached Bolinas Ridge. We had heard many tales of the wonderful view to be obtained from there, and reaching the western brow of the mountain, we forgot our hunger and fatigue when its wondrous beauty burst upon us. Far beneath us, stretching as far as the eye could reach, lay the silver ocean, while above it in the azure sky hung the sun, a brilliant ruby. Afar off in the hazy distance the Farallones rose out of the crystal sea, the one dark spot on the brilliant scene. The sky was spotted with fleecy clouds, tinted a delicate pink by the setting sun. Faintly every now and then we heard the boom of the waves as they broke upon the rocky shore. One could gaze for hours at the scene, but time will tarry for no one. All too soon the sun sank into his couch of fiery clouds ; all too soon the sea doffed his garb of silver hue for one of somber green. And so we left the ocean to the night, with that sunset scene so impressed on our memory that I doubt if any one of us will ever forget it.

GRACE SHAW.

Girls' High School, written in Class.

MAUDE E. HAMMOND.

THE CALIGRAPH.

TO the busy man of to-day one of the most important parts of his office paraphernalia is his typewriter, whether he be lawyer or judge, preacher or merchant, governor or mayor. In fact hardly an occupation in life could conveniently do without the machine or its work.

In an article of necessity of this kind, several points have to be taken into consideration by people about to purchase. One point, and that a most important one, is that of " speed "; another that of " wear "; while still another, that of ease of manipulation. These points are of vital importance, for it is evident to the merest beginner that a machine that is slow— one that is quickly worn so as to interfere with its work, or one that is difficult or unhandy to manage—would be next to useless to a man in haste to attend to correspondents.

Well, if these points are requisite in a typewriter, how are we to decide between the numerous patterns we see advertised which all claim everything possible in favor of their particular machines ? might be asked by a person in need of one. The answer is an easy one. They should profit by the experience of others and satisfy themselves as to which machine is the most used by people or firms competent to decide. If this common-sense method of selection is followed there is but one course to be pursued, and that is to buy a " Caligraph," because : Firstly, it possesses the qualifications in an eminent degree. Secondly, when such offices as the Pacific Postal Telegraph Company, who alone use twenty Caligraphs ; the Western Union Telegraph Company, who use them exclusively, as well as nearly every " telegraph office " on this coast ; when hundreds such people as R. H. Marling, A.M., Stenographer Executive Department; L. W. Storror, Superintendent Postal Telegraph Company ; Samuel W. Backus, Postmaster San Francisco ; M. C. Hunt, Manager Postal Telegraph Company, and many more of the most prominent business and professional men endorse it as being the fastest, most simple and most durable machine in the market, and will use no other, it is seen that the " Caligraph " is certainly the machine to buy.

The "Caligraph" has been before the people twelve years, and is handsomely made. The styles are varied, and the prices, considering the quality, are very low.

MAUDE E. HAMMOND,

2033 Howard Street.

Mission Grammar School, 8th Grade.

The above writer won the First Prize awarded by Chas. E. Naylor.

Photography.

PHOTOGRAPHY is an art. Although it would be difficult to set a date when what is known as " photographic action " was first recorded, it is commonly believed that Scheele, a Swedish chemist, was the first to experiment on the darkening effect of sun on chloride silver. To England belongs the honor of first producing a photograph by the use of Scheele's observations in 18c2. Daguerre was next to improve on Scheele's plan, but not until 1842.

Since then photography and its improvements have rapidly increased. Although progress has been rapid, it is only a short time since dry plates took the place of the wet process. Miles A. Seed was the originator of the dry process. Dry plates are now extensively used with the many kinds of developer.

But even with all the improvements of the present age, the photographer's life is indeed an unquiet one. Let us take the amateur for example. First, of course, comes some one wishing their likeness. After a discussion of prices, a primping of bangs, and a changing of garments, the person is finally ready. The photographer then seats them, and after giving them their position tells them to look at the camera ; in doing so some squint while others open their eyes as wide as possible, and when proofs are made they resemble a stuffed image or a mummy more than an animated being.

Besides, it is very probable that the person will come on such a day that it is impossible to get good light, in this case a little strategy is often exercised. In order to retain the job, the photographer assures the person that it is a fine day for taking pictures, and after putting in an empty plate-holder and carefully pulling the slide, says to come next day for the proof ; of course, next day he says that it was no good, and after having left their deposit the person generally sits until good weather and good luck happen to come together.

Then the average person with their conceit makes the life of the photographer miserable, by declaring their " eyes, nose, mouth or bangs NEVER looked like that." Then the one who, enjoying his vacation, takes his camera expecting to get fine views and who returning home finds a running brook and a dining-room scene on the same negative. Then in developing how often the negatives cling passionately together.

MAUDE E. HAMMOND,
2033 Howard Street.

Mission Grammar School, 8th Grade.

The above writer won the prize awarded by Taber Photographic Co.

Biography—Maude E. Hammond.

IN introducing the Essays and Stanzas of the Pupils of San Francisco's Public Schools, we take pleasure in presenting a biography of the prize winner on two subjects, namely, Photography and "The Caligraph," Miss Maude E. Hammond, who was born in the city of San Francisco, California, on May 23, 1879.

The result of an early attendance at school and a persistent adherence to studious proclivities has brought her prominently before her classmates as a subject of intellectual criticism. At the age of six years she first embarked into school life at the Lincoln Primary, and at once exhibited a decided inclination to study.

At so tender an age few children show any other faculty than that of childish prattle ; but for this student a brilliant career was at once mapped out for her future, and all along the line of her school days her ability has been fully established.

Having had a yearly promotion from the Primary Grammar Schools, Miss Hammond will graduate in the class of '95 from the Mission Grammar School, under the able superintendence of Mrs. Nettie R. Craven, Principal. At this school she has always been foremost in her classes, and has shown a remarkable adaptation for essay writing.

We need not comment on the subject of our sketch other than mention, what her personal friends are familiar with, such as an admirable associate with a disposition of a congenial character, and that her popularity among her schoolmates and teachers has won for her an enviable position among them.

The offer of prizes by the merchants of this city for competitive essays on the separate industries of San Francisco immediately occupied her attention, and without delay she sent into the offices of the Publishers four lengthy essays on different subjects, the merit of which succeeded in carrying off two valuable prizes. This merit, in itself, establishes the fact that she is a tireless worker and an ardent student, capable of governing a successful future.

Her father, Samuel C. Hammond, and Laura E. Hammond, her mother, both of intellectural stock, arrived here in the sixties from the Eastern States, and the natural adaptability of his family soon gained for him a reliable position in the commercial world. This streak of intelligence is plainly visible in his daughter. Our best wishes are offered to Miss Hammond for a successful graduation.

Coal.

COAL, is a term now commonly used to denote all kinds of mineral fuel, though formerly applied to the glowing embers of wood, and more recently to charcoal. English and German writers, until a very recent date, treated of mineral fuel as pit coal, Stemkohle (stone coal), etc., but at the present time, when wood and charcoal are fast giving place to the mineral varieties of fuel, the term coal is limited to that class of this fuel in general use.

Under the term we may therefore embrace all classes of mineral fuel that will ignite and burn with flame or incandescent heat.

BEULAH STUBBS.

Hydrogenated coal is the strictly bituminous or caking kind, and the most available for production of coke. In this coal hydrogen is the predominating element in its gaseous or volatile constituents, though both oxygen and hydrogen are generally present in such coals in nearly equal part ; but when oxygen predominates to any great extent, the coal loses its adhering or coking quantities ; and when hydrogen is present in considerable quantities, coal is more or less fat or rich, according to the common expression. In connection with a large percentage of fixed carbon, four to five per cent. of hydrogen, with the largest amount of coke, but even six per cent. of hydrogen, with eight to ten per cent. of oxygen, fails to produce available coke. The term hydrogenated, therefore, denotes more clearly than any other of the numerous varieties of bituminous coals variously demanded coking, caking, fat, rich or close burning coals. They do not burn freely, but meet and run into a mass or cake, from which the violate parts are slowly burned leaving the coke in an incandescent state of fixed carbon, which has the properties of anthracite and burns much the same, though it is porous and easily ignited.

Oxygenated coal embraces the free-burning, non-caking varieties of bituminous coal, the block or furnace coals of our western bituminous fields, the so-called lignites of the Rocky

Mountains and the far West; some of the cannel varieties, most of the splint coals, and the hard or dry bituminous coal of the English mines. In this class of coal oxygen predominates in the volatile caking or meeting and adhering in mass. Of this kind there are two prominent varieties: One is comparatively hard and burns to ash without crumbling, and constitutes the blast furnace or block coal, and most of the cannel and splint coals. The other is soft, frequently hygroscopic; often heterogeneous in composition; divides both horizontally and perpendicularly by earthly impurities, and sometimes is a mass of semi-crystallized and loosely combined cubes. This kind disintegrates in the atmosphere or under high temperatures, and cannot be used in the blast furnace under these existing conditions.

The hard, impure anthracite of New England frequently contains from five to fifteen per cent. of water, while the soft tertiary coals of the West contain an equal amount of water; and the purest coal contains a small amount of hygroscopic matter. As a class, however, the more recent coals of jurassic and tertiary formations contain the largest amount of water; and to these we apply the term hydrated to distinguish them from the oxygenated, though the former contains even more oxygen than the latter.

BEULAH STUBBS,

2519 Pacific Avenue.

Pacific Heights' Grammar School, 6th Grade.

The above writer won the prize awarded by Charles R. Allen.

Apostrophe to the Daisy.

LITTLE pink-tipped modest flower
  Lying in your bed of green,
Kissed by dewdrops from the heavens,
  Made to brighten many a scene.

Thou who art so meek and humble,
  Cov'ring loved ones 'neath the sod,
Giving nature much of beauty,
  Truly you belong to God.

ELLA NEUWAHL.

Girls' High School, Written in Class.

Carpets.

HOUSTON COOK.

WHEN we enter almost any house one of the first things which we see is the carpet on the floor. Probably most of us do not stop to think how these carpets are made or where the material of which they are made comes from. Let us do so now.

First of all we ask ourselves, what are carpets made of? and we say wool and cotton; then the next question is, how are these obtained?

The wool is obtained from sheep. The cotton is obtained from the cotton plant which grows both in our country and many others, and which gives employment to the many men who pick it, and which also caused slavery, with the aid of the cotton-gin, in the early part of this century, to increase.

Then we think of the labor and time it takes to prepare this cotton and wool for weaving, and the time and men it takes to weave it, and finally of the nice, soft, pretty carpets we see all over our home, and which give us so much comfort and warmth.

There are many different kinds of carpets; there are Persian carpets which are made by the native women of Persia, and are the most beautiful in the world. The process of making a Persian carpet is very slow and requires a great deal of patience, and patience, as we all know, is a great virtue which many of us do not possess. Patience, Bishop Horne says: "Among all the graces that adorn a Christian soul, like so many jewels of various colors and lustre, against the day of her espousals to the lamb of God, there is not one more brilliant than patience." Shakespeare says: "How poor are they who have no patience! What wound did ever heal but by degrees ?" The women are the only ones who weave the carpets, the men never touching them.

The Turkish carpets, are made by young girls in families, and made mostly of linen warp. Another kind is the Axminster carpet, which is an imitation of Turkish carpets, but is much handsomer, being made much more evenly ; they are made out of worsted.

There are also Brussels, Wilton, Tapestry and Kidderminster carpets ; the Kidderminster carpets being best known in this country as ingrain or three-ply carpets.

Carpets are one of the most useful articles in a home ; before they were known the people would weave grasses together and make rugs out of them.

The green, velvety grass often seen in the country reminds one of a velvety carpet such as we delight to walk on. In fact, we might call grass the carpet of the earth, with which nature has provided it to make it look beautiful. Goethe says of nature that it is, " The living, visible garment of God."

HOUSTON COOK,

141 Haight Street.

Denman Grammar School, 8th Grade.

Thoughts.

LET not thy thoughts dwell on the past,
  For of good deeds of men, I ween,
  We have not read or heard the last,
But many more will yet be seen.

Make it the aim of all your life
To strive for all that's good and right,
And if you win or lose the strife
Be ever noble in man's sight.

ESTHER R. WOLF.

Hamilton Grammar School, Written in Class.

GERTRUDE D. FEATHERSTONE.

Chocolate and Cocoa.

MANY long years ago in the far-away South
   Where the lovely cacao tree grows,
    At the very first note of the sweet-singing birds
The busy inhabitants rose.

An old Spanish house, built around a square court,
   Was the scene of much bustle and hum ;
For the day had arrived—that day of all days—
   For the chocolate woman to come.

Selecting one end of the court for herself,
   Protected from sun and the breeze,
She begins by roasting the cacao beans
   That are brought to her fresh from the trees.

When the beans are roasted a beautiful brown,
   She shells them with pains-taking care.
Then, of all the work of that busy day,
   She begins the most tiresome share.

Placing the beans on her grinding-stone,
   Which stands o'er a pan of hot coals,
She grinds them as fine as she possibly can
   With the "brazo" which heavily rolls.

Then an equal weight of sugar she adds
  And spices to suit the taste ;
And when these ingredients are thoroughly mixed
  They make a delicious brown paste.

She measures the paste with experienced hands,
  A pound in each little roll,
And spreads it out on an Indian mat,
  Into ounces dividing the whole.

Now, though she has labored from dawn until dusk
  Through the hours of that long, weary day,
She has made but ten pounds.   Could one expect more
  When made in that primitive way?

Now, if they wish a drink to prepare,
  One ounce for each cup they must take,
With water or milk in a " batador,"
  A pitcher of Indian make.

With a " molinilla," a fancy carved stick,
  They stir the mixture awhile,
And whirl it into a beautiful foam
  In the good old-fashioned style.

In our own fair land at the present time
  Stands a factory airy and vast,
Where a great many men are working each day
  With the aid of machinery fast.

Great quantities of the cacao beans
  Are roasted at once thoroughly ;
And then they are cracked and the shells blown away
  By the whirling machinery.

To prepare *cocoa* the oil is pressed out,
  From which cocoa-butter is made.
The remaining part is ground very fine,
  Thus forming the cocoa of trade

For *chocolate*, however, the oil is retained
  And the whole is pressed into a cake,
Which sweetened or not, as the case may be,
  Will many delicious things make.

When we think of the work that can be done
  In the modern and quicker way,
We are scarcely surprised to learn that they make
  Twenty-five hundred pounds in one day.

GERTRUDE D. FEATHERSTONE,
Girls' High School, Middle Class.   914 Twenty-fourth Street.
The above writer won the prize awarded by D. Ghirardelli & Sons.

Food and Medicinal Properties of Grapes.

OF all natural foods, grapes have probably the largest blood producing properties; and, since "The life of the flesh is the blood," it follows that as an all-round food they are not surpassed. There is less waste matter in grapes than in almost any other food. Indeed, if one swallow only the juicy matter between the rind and the stones he can digest and absorb into his body the greater part of it. This is a well known fact, for men have made chemical examinations of the blood and tissues of the body and also of the juice of the grape, and these are almost identical. Milk is the only other natural food that compares with grape juice in this respect.

JOHN COLBERT.

The California Grape Food Company took advantage of this quality in the grape and built extensive works at Los Gatos, California, where they separate the rind and stones and water from the "food" part, and bottle this and sell it to people to make them well if they are sick and to keep them well if they are well. It is so easily digested that the weakest stomach can use it. There is really no "work" for the stomach to do on this juice, for it is composed of blood, salts and grape sugar just as the blood is. It passes readily from the stomach to the liver, where it becomes "reddened" into blood. Even milk requires more "work" to make it into blood than does grape juice thus prepared.

Since the people in the Holy Land had this fruit given them in such abundance, one cannot help thinking that God gave it to them because it was so healthy and nourishing. He was their friend and gave them their food. But when men ferment the juice into wine that makes drunkards, they spoil its food properties ; this we can readily understand, since all dyspeptic or weak stomachs have too much fermentation already. It is the fresh grape juice that is the natural food.

As an aid in the sick room this prepared food is fast growing in popularity. I know a doctor who is now prescribing it for a sickly boy, who is improving every day since he began taking it. The little fellow's stomach was so weak that everything else but milk distressed him, and he even got tired of milk. Grape juice agrees with him and is building him up wonderfully.

As a communion wine it is destined at no distant date to occupy the whole field. It is the real fruit of the wine as God made it, and may therefore with safety symbolize the Savior's blood. Surely it was not grape juice that had rotted, or more politely "fermented," that was used by Christ on that memorable occasion when He said "This is my blood." No, it was fresh juice such as He makes in the grapes when they are growing.

JOHN COLBERT,
634 Elizabeth Street.

Lincoln Grammar School, 7th Grade.
The above writer won the prize awarded by The California Grape Food Co.

The Caligraph.

OF all the writing machines now before the public none is more widely or favorably known than the Caligraph. In every tournament where machines compete for prizes or distinction of any kind, this one is sure to enter and just as sure to win first place. Its speed far surpasses its competitors ; and somehow operators on it are also able to make a record for accuracy. In May, 1893, there was a tournament in New York, where many machines competed for a handsome gold medal offered by John W. Mackay. The Caligraph, of course, was there, and the result was that the other machines were " distanced," and the best of it was that the writers who won such laurels were gentlemen from this Coast, B. S. Durkee of Portland, and J. H. Jones of San Francisco. Mr. Durkee, who is now champion typewriter of the world, wrote the large number of ninety-seven telegraphic messages in sixty minutes. It took each of these young men only forty seconds to write every word on the message, including date, address, number, time and signature. How fast they must have worked, and how fast the Caligraph must have responded to the touch on its keys !

If we examine the construction of the Caligraph we can see good reasons for its supremacy in speed and accuracy. The level keyboard, with a key for every character, permits all writing to be done with the least waste of time and energy. The hand glides over it as over a piano. The type bars are so well balanced that the moment the finger strikes the key the type strikes the paper ; and they are so arranged that there is no danger of one type striking another when going fast.

The two spacing keys at the sides, instead of one at the bottom as in other machines, make the waste of time in spacing and the work of moving the hands much less.

Besides these special features there are many minor, but very important ones, in the Caligraph, which added together make it the champion in the field of writing machines. The attachments for receiving the paper, regulating the length of lines, regulating the spaces between the lines, and for correcting the errors, are all time-savers. The device of the Caligraph for keeping it in " alignment " after the wear and tear of time surpasses that on any other machine. The writer can tighten it up as it wears and thus keep it always like a new machine. Other machines are a total loss after they wear loose.

A gentleman who has been all his life engaged in Business College work, where they had all kinds of typewriters, advised me if ever I bought one to buy a Caligraph ; he said it did the fastest and best work, and would outlast any two others. He was not interested in any machine when he spoke of this to me.

JOHN COLBERT,

634 Elizabeth Street.

Lincoln Grammar School, 7th Grade.

The above writer won the Second Prize awarded by Charles E. Naylor.

The true purpose of education is to cherish and unfold the seed of immortality already sown within us ; to develop, to their fullest extent, the capacities of every kind with which the God who made us has endowed us.—MRS. JAMESON.

> 'Tis education forms the common mind,
> Just as the tree is bent, the twig's inclined.
> --POPE.

Arabian Coffee—Autobiography.

TO begin with the early part of my history, I must take you to a coffee plantation some fifty miles east of Damar. The plantation was owned by a rich old Arab, who had numerous slaves and servants, and made yearly pilgrimages to Mecca.

I was reposing serenely on the vine of my parent tree, one beautiful day in May, when I was rudely seized and jerked off the twig whereon I had staid for nearly three months.

When I recovered from the shock caused by my separation from the paternal tree, I found myself spread out on mats with millions of other little beans, and the sun beating down most unmercifully on our uncovered heads.

After being turned about in an endless and cruel manner, we were at last gathered up and transported to another building. Here we were passed between huge rollers, and when I emerged from the formidable looking monster, I noticed that my dry pulp which had inclosed my body, was gone. This knowledge did not alarm me ; in fact, I was rather glad to get rid of my surplus clothing, as the thermometer marked ninety degrees in the shade.

For two days I lay sweltering in that drying house ; we were then placed on the back of a camel and conveyed to Mocha.

From Mocha to London our journey was uneventful, and from London thence to New York. We were changed and tugged about in New York in an aimless manner, but at last were placed on the cars, bound for San Francisco, where we arrived in due season.

My next experience was in a roasting oven in a wholesale establishment on Front street. There I was simply cremated, and when I emerged from the oven I was browner than the proverbial berry.

From the wholesale house to a retail store was my next destination, and I had hardly been installed in my new quarters before I was purchased by a lady, who took me to her home in the " Western Addition."

I now supposed that my troubles all were over, so imagine my dismay when she placed me in a little mill and began turning the handle. I commenced sinking down, and ere long seemed to be being torn to shreds. Soon I was so thoroughly dissected that my best friend would not recognize me.

At present I am lying in a little can, preparatory to being boiled. What my next experience will be I am at a loss to know, nor do I care much, as my life has been so full of troubles.   WILLIE D. WARD,

Mission Grammar School, 8th Grade.   242 12th Street.

3

Statuary.

A THING of beauty is a joy forever," and this applies particularly to statuary.

Statuary is by no means of modern origin, as many different pieces have been unearthed from time to time, proving that they were many thousand years old. A notable example of this is the Egyptian Sphynx and other ancient pieces.

Italy and France are noted for their fine statuary; the former for marble and the latter for bronze.

America is not as yet far advanced in this art, but it is to be hoped that, as the country grows, it will progress in this, as it has done in many other things.

A great deal of statuary is imported to the United States, and many beautiful homes are embellished by it.

The very finest examples of this art, coming from all parts of the world, were exhibited at the World's Columbian Exposition. They were too numerous to mention, and I had the rare treat of viewing them.

The immense crowds which continually thronged the Building of Fine Arts, where the statuary was exhibited, showed the great appreciation of the public, and it proved the best education to the people.

Our own Midwinter Fair also had some fine subjects in statuary, among which was a group of the Vanderbilt family of New York, also some fine Japanese bronzes, several of which have been purchased, and will remain in the Art Building and form the nucleus of the museum into which the Art Building is to be converted.

BLANCHE M. STERNHEIM,

1728 Bush Street.

Denman Grammar School, 8th Grade.

Apostrophe to the Moon.

MOON, great orb of the reflected fire
That lights the world, when sinks the setting sun,
My bosom fills with envy more than ire,
To think of thee, the great and only one
Who, at thy wish, can get sublimely full.
Though others of their cash may be bereft,
Thou canst always take another great, long pull,
And still, O Moon, thou has a quarter left.

Girls' High School, Written in Class.   ALICE CHALMERS.

Benefits of the Installment Plan.

THE room was dark, but there sat within
  A woman, pale, haggard and thin,
    In her arms she caressed a baby boy,
And it seemed to be her only joy.
The woman said, as she caressed her babe,
That happiness o'er her home ne'er had strayed.

I asked her to state the reason why,
And she told me then with a sad, deep sigh,
That for years she had toiled so hard and long
To gain the comforts of a home,
And she never thought she would see the day
When she hadn't a place for her babe to lay.

But now she was greatly in need of a cot,
But how to get it, the way she knew not.
She hadn't the money ready at hand,
So I mentioned to her the Installment Plan.
I never heard of that, she said,
As she slowly raised her wearied head.

Oh! then I smiled and quickly said
Have you of this great plan never read,
How it aids many persons who now will take heed,
By small payments get that which they need,
Household goods and clothes beside,
There is hardly an article that is denied.

In another week I visited their home,
And found that happiness was there alone
With its welcome beams. But what was the reason?
The Installment Plan had brought this joyful season.
Oh! dear friends, this is not the only home
Where the Installment Plan's benefits are quickly shown.
There are thousands of homes that this way seem
Just as happy, all on account of this wonderful scheme.

AGNES CORRIGAN,

2307 Mariposa Street.

Mission Grammar School, 7th Grade.

Indian Rubber.

ONE of the great commodities of the world is rubber, because of the many uses to which it can be applied.

The first notice of rubber on record by Europeans was given nearly five hundred years ago by Herrera, who in the second voyage of Columbus observed that the inhabitants of Hayti played a game with balls made of the gum of a tree, and that the balls were lighter, though larger, than the wind-balls of Castile. In 1615 he published a paper with an account of rubber.

The caoutchouc-yielding trees are found in British India, the eastern shore of Africa, and South America, flourishing best on the rich alluvial banks of rivers in South America. South America yields nearly three-fourths of all the rubber used in the world.

The sap is collected in the dry season between August and February. The trees are tapped in the evening and the juice collected on the following morning. To obtain the juice a deep horizontal incision is made near the base of the tree, and then from it a vertical one extending up the trunk with others at short distances in oblique directions. Small shallow cups made from a clayey soil are placed below the incisions to receive the juice. The tree yields about six ounces of juice in three days. To obtain the rubber the juice is heated in the following manner: A piece of wood about three feet long with a flattened clay mould at one end is dipped in the milk. The milk is carefully dried by turning the mould round and round in a vapor obtained by heating certain oily palm nuts. Each layer of rubber is allowed to become firm before adding another. The rubber thus prepared is the finest that can be obtained.

We are much indebted to Mr. Goodyear for the invention of vulcanizing rubber which widely extended its usefulness. He experimented six years, and at last found that by mixing the rubber with sulphur and heating it to a great degree made it flexible.

It would be impossible to mention rubber's various uses. Belting, buffers, wheel-tires, washers, valves, pipes, fire-hose and other engineering appliances form a large branch of the rubber trade. Air-goods and water-proof cloth are made by placing layer after layer of india rubber paste on textile fabrics. There are between four hundred and six hundred rubber factories in England.

AGNES SCHUMACHER,
1223 Pierce Street.

South Cosmopolitan Grammar School, 7th Grade.

Chocolate and Cocoa.

A COCOA plantation is set in quite the same manner as an apple orchard, except that the young stalks may be transplanted from the nursery after two months' growth. Between rows and at like spaces are planted rows of Bucare, a tree of rapid growth that serves to shade the soil as well as to shield the young trees from the torrid sun. At the age of five years the plantation begins to bear fruit, and annually yields two crops that ripen in June and December.

In gathering, care must be taken to cut down only fully ripened pods. The pods are left in a heap for about twenty-four hours. They are then cut open, and the seeds are taken out and carried in a basket to the place where they undergo the operation of sweating or curing.

There the acid juice is first drained off, after which they are placed in a sweating-box and allowed to ferment, great care taken to keep the temperature from rising too high. The fermenting process is in some cases effected by throwing seed into holes or trenches in the ground and covering them with earth or clay. The seeds in this process, which is called claying, are occasionally stirred to keep the fermentation from proceeding too violently.

The sweating is a process which requires the very greatest attention and experience, as on it, to a great extent, depends the flavor of the seeds and their fitness for weather ; but a period of about two days yields the best results. Thereafter the seeds are exposed to the sun for drying and those of a fine quality should then assume a warm, reddish tint, which characterizes beans of a superior quality.

The seeds of the chocolate plant are brought into market in their crude state as almond-shaped beans, which differ in color and somewhat in texture.

The dried seeds have a papery, brittle shell, which is very smooth on the inside, but on the outside exhibits under the microscope a few short hairs and round excrescences.

In preparing cocoa beans for use, they are first roasted like coffee beans, then they are bruised and cleaned of the husks. The husks which are thus parted are the cocoa shells of commerce and the beans broken into pieces are called "cocoa-nibs." This is the purest form in which cocoa comes.

The paste that is made by grinding the nibs alone is properly called cocoa, and that made by grinding them with other substances and flavors, chocolate.

MAMIE KENNEDY,
318 Hill Street.

Franklin Grammar School, 6th Grade.

Advantages of a Business Education.

IN ALL times and even at the present moment, in education, people do not consider what is the most practical branch and useful one in the end, but what branch of education is considered the best by society. There are many things worth spending time upon in order to know them, but, in practice, and not in theory, there is no education to equal a business one ; and, in order to be a thorough business man or woman, one must have as fine a course of instruction in that line as a lawyer requires in his profession or an architect in his.

Science controls the day; there is nothing we do that does not contain the elements of science in its nature, although we may not know it ; so it is in business ; there is a science to it, and, unless one is instructed in it, he or she cannot make a master business man or woman.

We read of frauds and robberies committed by the very clerks, themselves, in an establishment that is considered first-class, and why ? Simply because the proprietors are poor managers and do not understand thoroughly how to conduct a business. Had they been educated, all evils would be avoided and a systematic business be carried on as a result of a good business education. Not alone is good management requisite in a business, but each separate branch must be conducted perfectly by thoroughly trained business men ; the stenographer, the cashier, the bookkeeper, the clerks, all must have their own special work at their finger tips, and, therefore, should have a complete education in their own work. I advocate strongly a good business education for both men and women, whether or not they intend leading a mercantile life. Who can say what may come to them in the vicissitudes of life ? and, in time of emergency, of what avail are the classics or mathematics compared with a knowledge of business dealings ? Then, if a woman is educated along that line, may she not exert a powerful influence upon her husband who has not such a vast education on the subject ?

I say a business education is highly necessary, and let the boys and girls have it, but do not allow them to go to poor schools, for a poor one is worse than none at all.

MIRIAM B. LEVY,

1501 Scott Street.

Graduate Girls' High School, Class '94.

Bohemian Coffee.

COFFEE is the seed contained in the berry of an evergreen shrub which grows in hot countries.

The shrub flourishes best in moist air and well-drained soil ; accordingly the hill-slopes of the islands of the two Indies are found especially suited to its cultivation.

The coffee plant prunes down to a height of five or six feet, so that it may bear better fruit and hold that fruit within easy reach.

The ripening coffee berry has a bright red color, and looks something like a cherry, but day by day its hue changes till at last it becomes a lovely deep purple. The berry is very sweet as it is, and palatable. But it is not for its sweetness that the coffee plant is grown ; it is for the sake of the two hard oval seeds which lie close together at the berry's heart.

These seeds are flat on one side and rounded at the other ; they lie with their flat faces towards each other, and are surrounded by a kind of tough husk which separates them from the juicy substances of the berry.

When the berries are ripe they are spread out in the sun to dry, being turned from time to time, till the pulp is shriveled up into a kind of pod. This pod is removed by hand, and what remains of the dried-up pulp is washed away. There are now left only the coffee beans, as they are called, and the tough shell or case in which they are hidden from sight. These shells are broken by means of wooden rollers, all the chaff is winnowed away, and the coffee is ready at last to be packed in sacks, conveyed to the nearest seaport, and shipped to the markets of the world.

Great care must be taken now to keep it separate from all articles having any strong odor, for coffee readily absorbs the odor of other substances. A few bags of pepper have been known to spoil a whole cargo of it.

Before the coffee can be put upon the table it must be roasted chestnut brown, ground in a coffee mill, and steeped in boiling water. Most of us would wish to sweeten it, too, and add a little milk, though some coffee drinkers prefer their coffee straight.

EMIL DOLD,

262 Eighth Street.

Franklin Grammar School, 6th Grade.

Drugs.

UNDER drugs we understand, generally, substances used for the cure of ailments, though spices and coloring matter are also included under that name.

There are vegetable, mineral and animal drugs. The first are obtained from plants of which the bark, the leaves, the roots and the seeds are used. They are employed in the shape of teas, tinctures, extracts and oils. Quite a number of these are used in the arts for tanning, dyeing and other purposes. The mineral drugs are derived from the mineral kingdom in which, at present, sixty-four elementary bodies are recognized. Fifty of these belong to metals proper. Through chemical reaction, mixture and combination the great number of chemicals are produced which are employed in medicine, as well as the arts.

In the way to illustrate which drugs are obtained from the animal kingdom, I shall mention a few and their source. Animal charcoal, for instance, is obtained by burning bones, and is, therefore, called animal charcoal. It is mainly used in sugar refineries for filteration. Pepsin, so greatly used in medicine, is obtained from the glandular layer of fresh stomachs from healthy pigs. The Cochineal is an insect found wild in Mexico and Central America, inhabiting different kinds of cactus plants. It is used for red coloring.

Having thus endeavored to describe to you what is meant by the term of drugs I close, hoping that I have succeeded to some extent.   RAE FLATOW,
                              810 Hyde Street.
South Cosmopolitan Grammar School, 8th Grade.

Why the Stars Twinkle.

WHY do the stars wink their eyes so bright
    When one looks into their faces at night?
    They seem to nod their heads of gold
And look at one with a countenance bold.

Perhaps it's because Mr. Moon is expected,
Or, maybe he's out, and must not be neglected ;
So they counsel together and wink their bright eyes,
While planning for him some pleasant surprise.

                    TINA RICHARDSON.
Girls' High School, Written in Class.

The Grape.

OH ! LUSCIOUS berry of the noblest lands,
  Product of all the climes that perfumes breathe,
  Nature salutes thee, and with eager hands
Would thee with crown of thine own glory wreathe.

Nor yields the gifted soil a richer tithe ;
  The golden fields bent 'neath their precious weight,
The very essence, nay, the germ of life ;
  These only can their treasures equal rate.

The subtle fragrance of thy clust'ring vines
  Brings grateful balm to parched and longing lips ;
It cools the fevered brow, and smooths the lines
  Of Pain, when that dread Monarch regal sits.

To health and joy thou lend'st a brighter hue,
  Thy pleasant fruit, a source of sweet delight ;
Thou temp'st the palate that thou seem'st to sue
  To taste of thy delicious fulsome wright.

E'en great Osiris, idol of the Nile,
  Hath prized the sweet aroma of thy fruit ;
Nay, Israel's Patriarch of the floating Isle
  Oft quaffed the must of thy most generous root.

And yet thou hast thy stern and austere foes,
  That reck not of thy good, thy cause abuse,
Such erring minds see but the frenzied throes,
  Of those, who wantonly, God's gifts misuse.

JENNIE SCHWARZSCHILD,
2015 Buchanan Street.

Graduate of Denman School, 1894.

Groceries.

A LARGE portion of food eaten by us consists of groceries. At every meal there are groceries on the table in some shape, either as salt, pepper, tea, coffee, sugar, or in some other form.

Tea, one of the most common of groceries, is used by almost every one. A great amount of the tea used in the United States is imported from China. There are different kinds of tea, such as comet, English Breakfast, uncolored Japan, green tea, etc.

Coffee is commonly used for breakfast, and a great many Germans use it with every meal. Mocha and Java are the finest kinds of coffee. Java is raised on the island of Java in the West Indies.

Sugar, which is exported from Honolulu and other places that have warm climates, is a great necessity. It is used to sweeten tea, coffee, preserves and a great many cooked articles. Four kinds of sugar are, granulated, powdered, loaf and brown sugar. Although there is not so much difference in the taste of sugar, there is a great deal of difference in its appearance.

Spices, such as nutmeg, cloves and cinnamon, are always convenient to have in the house, as they are often used to improve the taste of food.

Flavoring extracts are in much demand, especially to people who do much cooking in the line of pies and puddings. Vanilla, lemon and pineapple are three different flavoring extracts.

Condiments—tomato catsup, Worcestershire sauce, pepper sauce, pickled onions, caper sauce, pickles, pickled mushrooms and chow-chow, give a great deal of flavor to anything they are eaten with, especially cold meats.

Canned fruits, jellies and jams are used a great deal in winter, as they are much cheaper than butter.

There is also cocoa and chocolate. To make a delicious drink on a rainy day there is nothing tastes better than chocolate or cocoa. Then a few high-tea cakes, or cocoanut cakes, chocolate wafers, or any of those fancy cakes that can be bought in a grocery store, go very nicely with it.

Dried fruits, such as dried pears, apples and peaches, can be obtained all the year round, and stewed they make a very good dessert.

There are numerous other things in the line of groceries that when eating them we do not think of their importance, but if they could not be obtained they would be missed greatly.

JULIA BYRNES,

Mission Grammar School, 8th Grade.   37½ Russ Street.

Italian Paste, Vermicelli and Macaroni.

FLOUR is first brought downstairs by means of a chute. Then three one-hundred-pound sacks are put into a mixing machine and a pail of boiling water and a pail of cold water is added. The flour and water are left in this mixing machine about twenty-five minutes.

When the flour and water have been thoroughly mixed, they are taken out through a door in the bottom of this machine and put in a large sort of tub, in which it is rolled by a marble millstone. This millstone turns around and crushes all the little lumps of flour that may be in it. Then it is put in a machine with a mold at the bottom, and one machine makes Macaroni and the other Vermicelli.

This Macaroni and Vermicelli is cut into lengths of about one yard long and put on trays and sent upstairs into a room that is filled with steam, in order to make it tough. Then it is put into another room with a little air and a good deal of steam in order to make it a little harder. After this still it is removed to another room to finish it.

The Italian paste consists of little designs, letters and figures cut out of the flour.

It takes 1,200 lbs. of hydraulic pressure to make Vermicelli and 1,000 lbs. of hydraulic pressure to make Macaroni. In making the yellow Macaroni and Vermicelli the yolk of egg and saffron are used. Macaroni, Vermicelli and Italian paste are used for food, for soup, etc.

The stamps that mold the Macaroni, Vermicelli and Italian paste are made of copper, with the design wanted stamped on them. After being used, these stamps are put in water and thoroughly cleaned for use the next time they are wanted. The whole stamping outfit is called the pastile. The boxes for the Macaroni, Vermicelli and Italian paste are made in the factory, but downstairs. First the wood is chopped by means of a machine with something like a wheel and an edge like a saw. This cuts the wood as it is pushed through; then by means of another machine the board is evened off. The sides and ends are put together by means of another machine. One side and one end are taken and a piece for the foot is pressed upon and two nails are put in at once ; then the bottom is put on ; then the boxes are put in an intensely heated, airtight room, so that the boxes may be thoroughly dried, because the Macaroni, Vermicelli and Italian paste would get sour if they were not dry.   LUCY L. DUNNE,

912A Larkin Street.

Denman Grammar School, 8th Grade.

Jewelry.

IT IS said that every class of people of which any mention is made, from the savage to the civilized, have had a fondness for jewelry. History tells us that no matter how rude or humble the race or tribe was, their vanity found pleasure in personal adornment.

The first jewelry worn was made from natural objects, such as small shells or pebbles, dried berries, colored feathers and claws of wild beasts, strung together in some outlandish manner, and worn on the head, neck, arms and legs, the fingers and toes, ears and nose of the braves and dusky maidens.

Longfellow, in "The Song of Hiawatha," writes of the lament of the ancient arrow maker, after Hiawatha had carried off his charming daughter, Minnehaha:

> "Comes a youth with flaunting feathers,
> Beckons to the fairest maiden,
> And she follows where he leads her,
> Leaving all things for the stranger!"

The advocates of Delsartism went the savages one better, and introduced rings for the thumbs.

In the Bible it speaks of the golden calf that Aaron made out of the golden earrings taken from the wives, sons and daughters of the children of Israel, and how they worshiped this calf until Moses came down from the mountains, and, in his indignation at witnessing such a spectacle, took the calf and burnt it in the fire, then ground it to powder, and put it upon the water, and made them drink of it.

Probably that is where the saying originated of "tasting the gold in their drink."

The manufacture of jewelry reached a high state of perfection under the Egyptians, while the Greek and Roman jewelry is said to be unsurpassed by our modern workmen.

Modern jewelry is divided into three classes, viz:

I.   Objects in which gems form the principal part.

II.   When the metal is the most important part, used with gems.

III.   When the metal is used alone.

ADAH E. HORR,
2207 Webster Street.

Pacific Heights School, 7th Grade.

Pure Paints.

PURE paint was perfected only in very late times.

The art of architecture is very old, and is derived from the ancient Greek, Roman and Gothic models. They have never been improved, and perhaps never will be. But one thing that has been greatly improved upon is the paint, which gives the houses of the present time a very artistic appearance.

In ancient times they had a very rude sort of paint, but in later years it has been wonderfully improved by combining several colors together, and this gives it a very beautiful effect.

Pure paint consists of one-half zinc, one-half lead, mixed with pure linseed oil. This is passed through three powerful sets of mills and six powerful mixers. This mixing takes twelve hours.

Lead gives hardness and a glossy appearance. Zinc enables the paint to spread well. The mixing gives spreading properties, great body and elasticity.

Pure paints contain pure white lead, pure oxide of zinc, pure coloring pigments and pure linseed oil. Lead and oil alone would make a paint too soft, and it would chalk too easily. Zinc alone would be too hard.

Pure paint contains no water, benzine, barytes, whiting or other adulterants.

There are forty different shades for houses, which have been obtained by long experience.

Pure paint is the most durable and most beautiful paint known. Two coats of it will last well for five years. It is used for outside and inside work, for painting plastered walls, for floors, for tin and shingled roofs, and many other things. It is differently mixed according to the surface to be painted.

ANNIE RAUER,

South Cosmopolitan Gram. School, 7th Grade.   1120 Ellis Street.

If I were an Artist, what I would Paint.

WERE I an artist, I would paint
Some pure madonna, or a saint,
A scene of mount, of brook or hill,
A noisy, babbling little rill.
A glimpse of home, from cares all free,
And baby asleep on papa's knee,
With face of innocence, peace, repose,
And such, that none but an artist knows.

Girls' High School, Written in Class.   EDA COBLENTZ.

Photography.

PHOTOGRAPHY, like other branches of chemistry, owes its origin to the alchemist, who in his fruitless researches after the Philosopher's Stone and Elixir Vitæ, produced a substance to which he gave the name of Luna Cornea or Horn Silver, which was observed to blacken on exposure to light. This property of the substance constitutes the leading fact upon which the science of photography is based. The honor of having been the first to produce pictures by the action on a sensitive surface is now very generally conceded to Thomas Wedgwood. In 1814 a process called heliography was accomplished by Mr. Niepce. This process consisted in coating a piece of plated silver or glass with a varnish made by dissolving powdered asphaltum to saturation in oil of lavender, taking care that the drying and setting of this varnish be allowed to take place in the entire absence of light and moisture. The plate so prepared was then exposed in the camera obscura for a length of time varying from four to six hours, according to the amount of light given. A process called "Dry Collodion Process," was to wash off the free nitrate from the surface and allow the film to dry in the absence of light. A number of sensitive plates can be prepared by this method in anticipation of a journey. A late improvement in the preparation of the glass for a negative consists in giving it a thin coat of albumen on the side which is to receive the collodion. The practice of photography in the present day is confined almost exclusively to the Positive, the Negative and the Dry Collodion Processes. The Positive is to obtain in the camera a direct image, which is to be viewed by reflected light; and as it is desired that the pictures so produced should possess pure blacks and whites, an inorganic (nitric) acid is used in the bath and the developer; protosulphate of iron is also of inorganic origin, these being the conditions best calculated to produce a deposit of pure white metallic silver. In the Negative process, however, an image possessing density to transmitted light is required; accordingly an organic (acetic) acid is used, both in the bath and developer; and in order still further to insure an efficient supply of organic matter to combine with the silver at the moment of its reduction, pyrogallic acid is sometimes exclusively used.

RAY OPPENHEIMER,

1534 O'Farrell Street.

Hamilton Grammar School, 8th Grade.

The Birthday Gift.

BEND your head down close to mine
While I tell to you a secret fine.
 You must solemnly promise it to keep,
Else, I won't tell it to you, my sweet.

Mamma's birthday is coming very soon
And I only ask of you this boon,
That to us your presence you will lend,
If I to you an invitation send.

Now I hope you will not give away
The present we are to give that day.
We saved and planned it so well,
And then we left it to Sister Belle.

She went to work without delay
And searched and hunted for many a day
To find a gift that health and rest could give,
And last as long as one would live.

We love her so, there's nothing too fine
To give to this darling mother of mine.
So this present, fit for any queen,
She is to have a *Sewing Machine.*

How glad she'll be, what sewing she'll do
For us children all – may be something for you,
For the machine sews, ruffles, embroiders so fine,
There is not a machine so good in the line.

No machine with it can even compare,
And none have I heard ever did dare ;
So Belle has, I am sure, made the very best choice ;
That we all say with one glad voice.

Don't forget ; be sure to remember
The birthday comes on the first of September.
Send the machine to our number and street.
And we will give it a welcome sweet.

HAZEL A. BROWN,
2911 Deakin Street, Berkeley.

Le Conte School, 6th Grade.

Statuary.

WHAT a mine of interest the very name brings to mind! If these figures of marble and china, the forms of clay and shapes of brass, could have the gift of speech for one day, what stories we should hear!

Who has not seen statues of Venus, Mars, Cupid, and all the other Greek gods and goddesses? From the earliest period of paganism the people fashioned statues of their favorite deities. In the ruins of the buried cities of Pompeii and Herculaneum statues and statuettes are being constantly unearthed. Nearly everyone has seen copies of the celebrated Greek statue of Venus. Venus was the goddess of beauty. The statue is considered perfect in proportion. It is also thought to be the natural outline of the female form.

England also has many beautiful statues, both ancient and modern. If the statues in Westminster Abbey could be imbued with life, they would be much surprised to find themselves in such a place and among such queer associates.

Leaving England and coming to the United States, the first statue we think of is that of George Washington. What American does not feel patriotic when he sees on a public square the statue of our greatest hero!

It seems strange to us to think that while Italy and France, indeed all Europe, were making statues and painting pictures, our own country remained undiscovered.

Talking about our country reminds me of the person who found our land. What would Columbus think if his statue had come to life while the World's Fair was going on? He would have been much astonished, to say the least, at the place in which he would have found himself. All the great buildings and their contents would sadly confuse him.

Nearly all the sculptors who desire to become masters of their art go to Italy for a course of study. France also has many beautiful works of art. Her public gardens and boulevards usually contain many statues.

Spain's statuary is mostly religious in character. The most noted Italian sculptor was Michael Angelo, who did much to improve the art.

The noted French sculptors now living are David D'Angers, Pradier and Clesinger.

Olin Warner is one of the noted American sculptors. He was born in Connecticut about forty years ago. He modeled many beautiful things for the Centennial Exposition (1876).

JULIA CUNNINGHAM,

Mission Grammar School, 8th Grade.   322 Eighteenth Street.

The Little Brook.

AMID the woodland's shady dells
 A little brook its story tells ;
 And bending silently so near
Tall elder trees stoop low to hear.

By banks of gay free flowers
This little brook runs on by hours ;
And as it flows on to the sea
It sings a song to you and me.

Little birds from their shady nook
Hover o'er this running brook ;
And as it passes over ferns
The miller's wheel it quietly turns.

Through many a quaint old town it passes
Where live people of all classes.
It takes in every thing in motion
Until it reaches the dark blue ocean.

ELSIE SILVA.

Written in Class.
Girls' High School.

Apostrophe to the Moon.

OH ! Beautiful moon !
 May thy silvery light
 Guide spotted mortals' steps aright.
Send, always send, thy silvery aid,
That we may ne'er be lost in shade,
For thou, that rulest waves and tide,
Shall not forsake this land, our pride ;
And if thou should'st but one may know
Where on this flying path we go.

FLORENCE SOLLMAN.

Girls' High School, Written in Class.

4

HAZEL A. BROWN.

Groceries.

IN every, country, State and clime,
  Groceries are needed all the time.
Where, the freshest and best of them to find,
Is ever the wish and study of mankind.

Blest is the firm who, with the greatest of ease,
Has found the way the people to please.
The grocers, Goldberg, Bowen and Lebenbaum,
Have joined together and found the charm.

The very moment they open their doors,
Into them trade from everywhere pours.
Men and women are ashamed to own
That they never heard of Lebenbaum & Bowen.

All know, of grocers, they take the lead,
For half of the city they surely feed.
There's not a city, village or town,
But offer to them the enviable renown.

A short time ago they were separate firms,
But such a good name they both did earn,
That it was then decreed by fate
By all means they should consolidate ;

And thus build up a gigantic trade,
Where millions of dollars could be made.
And that this is just exactly right
Is proved by visiting the store some night.

The minute you enter the very door
You see many things you ne'er saw before ;
And whenever a trip through the store is paid,
You may well think a trip round the world you have made.

It is just like a tale from the Arabian Nights,
Everything is so beautiful—everything so bright.
You need but to express a wish or command,
And instantly a Genii will before you stand,

Ready to bring, at your will or pleasure,
From any land the rarest treasure ;
Exactly as if Aladdin's lamp you possessed,
And thus gained every wish you had expressed.

The groceries kept are always fresh and good,
And embrace every known article of food.
Barrels, boxes, casks, cases and crate,
Are coming and going from early till late.

The owners are men whom all do trust,
For they have been found honest and just.
So may Heaven bless and keep from harm,
Our grocers, Goldberg, Bowen & Lebenbaum.

HAZEL A. BROWN,
2911 Deakin Street, Berkeley.

Le Conte School, 6th Grade.

The above writer won the prize awarded by Goldberg,
Bowen & Lebenbaum.

" Sadly Left."

THREE little kittens in a kitchen were playing,
And in their kitten talk they were all saying :
" I wonder if we can't find something real nice,
Such as a great big bowl of milk with lots of rice ! "

Suddenly on the table they discovered a dish,
And thinking that in it were probably some fish,
They jumped up in a rush, all scrambling to see,
And found to their disgust nothing but " cold, cold tea."

JENNIE A. BURY.

Hamilton Grammar School, 8th Grade.

Carpets.

CARPET is a kind of woolen cloth used principally for the floors of apartments. It is made generally of wool, but is also made of cotton, hemp and straw. It is made in breadths to be sewed together and nailed to the floor, and is thus distinguished from a rug or mat.

In Egypt they were used first by the priests in the temples of religion, and in the palaces of the Pharoahs. The pre-eminence of the ancient Babylonian carpet weavers does not appear ever to have been lost sight of by their successors, and at the present time the carpets of Persia are as much prized and eagerly sought by European nations as they were when ancient Babylon was in the zenith of its glory.

Oriental carpets were first introduced into Spain by the Moors ; into France, during the reign of Henry IV, and later by the Venetians into Italy.

Persia is now, as it has been from the most remote period, the recognized source of what is truly artistic, durable and valuable in their manufacture.

In Persia there are entire tribes and families whose sole occupation is that of carpet weaving.

The greater portion of the real Turkish carpets imported into England are made by hand.

The manufacture of carpets is widely distributed throughout the East Indies. The weaving is carried on entirely by natives. There is considerable variety in the designs of Indian carpets, but it is allowed that they exhibit perfection of harmonious coloring.

The characteristic carpet weaving of Europe is entirely the product of machine or loom work, and of such there are several distinct varieties, namely: Kiderminster or Scotch, Brussels, Moquette, Wilton, Tapestry and Axminster.

In the United States the manufacture of carpet is very extensive and carried on to great perfection.

Carpets add greatly to the beauty of an apartment if taste is displayed in their selection. They should be darker in tone and more broken in hue than any other portion of a room that is fully furnished, because they present the largest mass of color and serve as a background to the furniture. Lighter carpets in more sparsely furnished apartments.

A better idea of the wonderful degree of perfection to which this branch of industry has reached could not be obtained than by a visit to any of the great carpet emporiums in our own city, where are to be found the choicest makes that the world produces, of every grade and texture, of every degree of price, from the highest to the lowest, all tastefully selected and artistically arranged, producing a harmony of shades that would fain entitle the admiration of the most fastidious.

LILLIE E. McGILL,

2200 Steiner Street.

Pacific Heights Grammar School, 8th Grade.

The above writer won the prize awarded by W. & J. Sloane & Co.

The Children in Our Block.

WE see them in the morning
    We see them late at night,
We see them all day Sunday—
    They are never out of sight.

They're laughing and they're shouting
    They're as noisy as can be;
They're always happy, never pouting—
    A frown you never see.

They are kind to those around them,
    They are kind to those they meet;
They are never mean or selfish—
    The children in our street.

GETTIE STODDARD.

Girls' High School, Written in Class.

Drugs.

FANNIE KINGSLAND.

DRUG is a name ordinarily applied to simple medicines, but by extension to every substance employed in the cure of disease. It is from the Teutonic *trocken*, "to dry." A drug may be an animal, vegetable or mineral substance.

In the earlier part of the world's history these substances in crude forms were applied to all altered conditions of the body constituting disease.

To the alchemist of old, however, is due the credit of making the first scientific investigations and discoveries, which have led up to the perfect knowledge of modern chemistry. Chemistry was virtually the art of extracting juices from plants for medicinal purposes.

It is to the perfect science of chemistry of to-day that we are indebted for the elegant and exact preparations of drugs, instead of the nauseating decoctions of early times.

The nicety and precision with which all drugs are now prepared and dispensed renders them palatable and pleasing in appearance, and robs them of their terrors when taken as a medicine.

Drugs when not properly used often do more harm than good. When necessary, which often happens, none but the best should be used, regardless of cost. Nothing should ever be too good or too costly for the sick. In order to procure the best only the largest and most complete establishments should be patronized, where every facility for the proper compounding of drugs is offered.

Drugs to exercise their full medicinal effects must be made fresh, from selected stock, in small quantities, and of standard strength. If long kept they become changed from the light, heat and evaporation, which would make some dangerous to use, while others would become practically inert.

The effect of drugs on the body, according to the kind used, ranges from a mild carminative to a most deadly narcotic. It would be well to remember also that no two drugs have exactly the same effect, and oftentimes the same drug has contrary effects in different persons.

FANNIE KINGSLAND,

1778 Green Street.

Pacific Heights Grammar School, 8th Grade.

The above writer won the prize awarded by Wakelee & Company.

The Land Where the Lost Things Go.

WHERE is the land where the lost things go ?
 Is it a country of rain and snow ?
 Or do tropic flowers bloom all the year?
And what is done with the lost things there ?

Could they know the grief of the little girl,
When Tommy or Jennie, Rosie or Pearl
Are lost, the heart of the child would be filled with joy,
By the quick return of her cherished toys.

Oh, cruel people in that unknown land,
Could you not keep your wicked hands
From mamma's thimble or baby's toy
And the precious tops of our darling boy ?

HELEN SIMMONS.

Girls' High School, written in Class.

Custom Boots and Shoes.

THE aches and pains which afflict humanity are very numerous, but there are none that cause more annoyance than those of the feet.

Corns, bunions and swelled joints are some of the complaints of the feet, and are in most cases the result of wearing for their covering something which has a tendency to gall, chafe or compress the toes, joints or heels in such a manner that every step causes unnatural friction, or a straining of the joints and cords.

JOHN E. BAKER.

Prevention is always better than cure for physical complaints, and to prevent these ailments of the feet, the parents of children should see that they have proper feet wear, made to conform to the natural construction of the foot.

If a person is unfortunate enough to have any of the various foot complaints, their only remedy is to have their shoes or boots made expressly to accommodate the afflicted parts.

It is therefore necessary, if we desire shoes that will be becoming in appearance and comfortable to wear, that we have them made by some one who can take the proper dimensions of the feet, show good judgment in the selection of material used, and be skilled in their construction, that they may be durable and give a satisfactory fit.

In measuring, a pencil mark is made around each foot on a piece of paper to learn the amount of space the bottom of the foot occupies ; then the dimensions in length are taken from heel to toe upon a measuring stick, and after that a tape measure is drawn over the foot at the ball, waist and instep.

With these measurements a pair of lasts can be fitted up that will conform to the right and left foot upon which the shoes are made.

From the last the pattern is draughted, and care must be taken to have the seams and ridges so located as to not interfere with tender or bending places of the foot.

The bottom of the shoe is made of sole leather and must be pliable and tough. The outside of the uppers is made from calf, kangaroo, goat and various other skins, which have been tanned into leather suitable for the part for which they are intended.

If the shoe is for easy indoor wear, the material is light and pliable ; but if the shoe is to be worn in rough places and subjected to a good deal of strain, they are made heavier.

The advantage of having custom-made shoes is that we can have them fit the feet, while if we buy them ready-made we must fit our feet to the shoes.

JOHN E. BAKER,

717 Eddy Street.

Clement Grammar School, 8th Grade.

The above writer won the prize awarded by John Utschig.

Our Family Cat.

A LOVABLE thing is our family cat,
　As she sleeps in the bright sunlight ;
But a hateful thing is the same old cat
　When she causes a concert at night.

A mild, gentle thing seems this quiet cat,
　When she basks in the firelight ;
But not quite so mild and gentle is she,
　When she starts in to scratch and bite.

Although she's only a little black cat,
　With white on her paws and breast,
We love her, and would not exchange her for
　The finest cat in the West.

MATTIE IJAMS.

Girls' High School, Written in Class.

Jewelry.

PERSONAL ornaments seem to have been among the very first objects on which the invention and ingenuity of man were exercised.

The granulations of surfaces practised by the Curuscans was long a puzzle and a problem to the modern jeweler, until Signor Castellani, of Rome, discovered gold workers in the Abrizzi, to whom the method had descended through many generations, and by inducing some of these men to go to Naples revived the art, of which he contributed examples to the London Exhibition of 1872, successfully applied to modern designs.

Modern jewelry may be classified under three heads : 1st, objects in which gems and stones form the principal portions, and in which the gold work is really only a means for carrying out the design, by fixing the gems or stones in a position arranged by the designs ; the gold being visible only as a setting ; 2nd, when gold work plays an important part in the development of the design, being itself ornamented by engraving or enameling or both, the stones and gems being arranged in subordination to the gold work in such positions as to give a decorative effect to the whole ; 3rd, when gold or other metal is alone used, the design being wrought by hammering in *repousse*, casting, engraving or chasing, or the surface left absolutely plain but polished and highly finished.

A design is first made on paper, drawn, or colored, and when needed with separate enlargements of details, everything in short to make the drawing thoroughly intelligible to the jeweler. According to the nature and purpose of the design, he cuts out, hammers, files and brings into shape the constructive portions of the work as a basis. Upon this, as each detail is wrought out, he solders or fixes by rivets the ornamentation necessary to the effect.

The human figure, representations of animal life, leaves, and fruit, are modeled in wax, moulded and cast in gold to be chased up and finished. As the hammering goes on the metal becomes brittle and hard, and then it is passed through the fire to anneal or soften it.

When stones are to be set, or when they form the principal portions of the design, the gold has to be wrought by hand so as to receive them in little cup-like orifices, the walls of gold enclosing the stone, and allowing the edge to be bent over to secure it.

Stones set in a slovenly manner, however brilliant in themselves, will look commonplace by the side of skillfully set gems of much less fine quality. Enameling has of late years taken the place of "paste" or false stones.

Engraving is a simple process in itself, and diversity of effect can be produced by skillful manipulation.

MINNIE JENNE,

247 Langton Street.

Franklin Grammar School, 8th Grade.

The above writer won the prize awarded by W. K. Vanderslice & Company.

The Stars.

"WHY is it the stars so twinkle?"
 Asked a child of three or four,
  While pride with joy was mingled
As she stood at the open door,
And gazed at the sky above her,
 Ablaze with heavenly light,
That never seemed to slumber
 But kept its watch all night.

"Because when baby's naughty,
 The Angels shut their eyes,
But ope them just as quickly
 At your fault, to hide surprise:
For when you slap poor brother,
 His eyes soon fill with tears
And his weak voice cries for pity,
 And comes to the Angels' ears."

CHRISTINA REGAN.

Girls' High School, Written in Class.

Photography.

IT is somewhat difficult to determine a date when photographic action originated. It may be supposed that Scheele, a Swedish chemist, was the first to discover that silver chloride could be darkened by the action of the sun.

England immediately took advantage of this discovery and claims the honor of producing the first photograph by the utilization of his observations.

The first one to design a process of photography, which gave pictures that were subsequently unchanged by light, was Nicephore de Niepce. His process consisted of coating the surface of a metallic plate with a solution, and exposing it to a camera image.

LILLIAN CLARKSON.

It is thought that a method will be discovered by means of which the colored rays that make up the white light may leave their respective colors on the sensitive surface; but at the present time this cannot be done, because these colors remain only a short time on the surface, being soon destroyed by the action of light.

The camera is the eye through which we see hundreds of places otherwise invisible to us. Its pictures are one of the greatest boons to the civilized world. By its aid the poor and the rich are alike amused. It enables us to partially enjoy the pleasure of traveling while we are in our own homes.

An Italian invented the first camera in 1540, which was useless, but it was the mother of the apparatus now in use. The camera of to-day is worked in this manner : A dark cloth is draped about it to lighten or darken the effect, and a lens is also moved back and forth. The image is taken on glass almost instantaneously, the exposure in some cameras being from five seconds to one one-hundredth of a second.

The negative or piece of glass on which the picture is taken is then developed, or goes through a chemical process by which the picture upon its surface becomes visible. Then the negative is placed over a piece of silvered paper, and both are fastened in a wooden frame so that the sun's rays may act upon them and cause the picture to appear on the paper. This paper is produced by moistening it with metallic silver. This does not change color in a dark place, but in the sunlight it becomes nearly black. The violet rays of the sun have the most influence on the image.

After being in the sunlight a short time the picture on the paper side is light gray, but the longer the sunlight acts upon it the darker it becomes, varying from a light brown to almost black. After the image is impressed upon the sensitized paper, it is removed from the frame and retouched.

Photography has been so improved that pictures are now taken while the object is in motion. The camera was modeled after the eye and has advanced with civilization, from the crude apparatus of early times to its present scientific state.

LILLIAN CLARKSON,

522 Eddy Street.

Denman Grammar School, 8th Grade.

The above writer won the prize awarded by F. H. Bushnell.

A Small Sister's Opinion of "Our Johnny."

OUR Johnny is the happiest boy
 In all this great wide town,
For Uncle Dave to-day gave him
 An ugly painted clown.

I couldn't love a piece of wood
 Just 'cause it talks like Poll,
And jumps and squeaks when it's touched—
 I'd rather love my doll.

ESTELLE BAKER.

Girls' High School, Written in Class.

Wellington Coal.

ONCE] upon a time way down in the deep dark earth, where "Old Sol," the Day King, never showed his bright face, a noble family of the ancient name, Wellington, ruled over all the coal-bearing regions. For many years this King Wellington's ancestors had ruled wisely and justly.

One day the king and his subjects were startled to hear a great, loud, rumbling noise in the distance. It came nearer and nearer, louder and louder,

MARY McKEON.

until—who can describe that moment ? the earth trembled and with a terrible noise it parted, and the light of day streamed into the dark palace of King Wellington.

The whole city was in a tumult to know the cause of the light, and crowds had gathered in the grand court of the palace. Looking upward they perceived a great golden ball far off, and the light, which had caused so much confusion, seemed to come directly from it.

The hard, black walls of the palace shone like gold in its rays. When the tumult had somewhat subsided, the people wisely went about their work, to await events. This state of affairs, however, did not last long, for very soon many queer little things dressed in black were walking over their heads and peering into the hole. Before long they had built long pieces of wood into the ground and were soon at work.

One morning the king and his people were surprised to see these black things coming down the pieces of wood. When they alighted they were all talking, and one man was heard to say, " That earthquake of yesterday has made us rich. This is a valuable mine of genuine Wellington coal, and we all know what *Wellington* means." Very soon the news of the discovery of the mine of Wellington coal—the joy of the household—spread like wild-fire over the country. In a short time many men were working with queer tools in the king's country. They tore down his palace, and his loyal citizens cried out, but their cries were buried in the crash with which the stately palace fell. Piece by piece it was put into a huge box, and the heart-broken citizens saw it hoisted high above their heads. After awhile it disappeared altogether, never to be seen again in that underground world. Nor did these greedy men stop here, but day after day the homes and families were broken up and carried away. It was my good luck to meet one day the father of one of these families of coal, who told me the sad way in which his family was broken up. He told me how he was put in a box with two of his children and a number of families which they knew, and carried away. They were put in a dark place in a large ship, which shook very much. We were glad to get on shore again, where we were put in a wagon and carried to a large house. Here our eyes were greeted by the welcome sight of piles of coal, but we were well able to hold ourselves above them all, for none of them bore the envied name—Wellington. Before long we were purchased by some man and brought to his house. The family were delighted by our warm, genial glow, and the husband declared he would never use any other coal.

MARY McKEON,

2116 Steiner Street.

Pacific Heights Grammar School, Graduate Class '94.

The above writer won the prize awarded by Thomas Morton.

Our Brave Heroes.

OH, ye brave, courageous heroes,
　From whom the tide of life hath fled,
　　But who in your time hath fought the foes,
　And among the thousands bled.

Forgotten ! your deeds shall be never,
　Nor your names e'er be effaced ;
But will keep their place forever
　In the hearts of our American race.

MABEL LEARY.

Girl's High School, Written in Class.

Rubber Goods.

WM. BORADORE.

THE method by which to utilize the catechu that was so abundant in the East Indies and in South America, had long been sought. Ships had brought it over as ballast from time immemorial, and one and another had attempted to render it useful in the manufacture of those articles for which it seemed so perfectly adapted, and which the world stood in need of.

France was the first to put it to any real use, not far from the year 1820, by weaving strands of the rubber with the goods for garters and suspenders ; and also to some extent for blacking and polish. The first pair of India-rubber shoes were exhibited in Boston in 1820, but they were what one would call monstrosities, and were looked upon merely as curiosities more than anything else. In the summer these melted, and the only thing to be done was to discover a process of preparation.

A process was discovered by Mr. Chaffee which was believed to be the best thing yet hit upon. Just as soon as the summer heat came his goods melted also, but this was not all, for they gave such an offensive odor that they were obliged to bury them.

A gentleman stepped into the warerooms of a company in Philadelphia only for curiosity, to inspect the rubber goods, and purchased a life preserver, which he examined carefully, and finding the valve clumsy and defective, he invented a better one, with which he hurried back to New York, hoping to sell it to some company. This man, born with genius stamped upon his brow and upon his soul, was Charles Goodyear.

Mr. Goodyear listened to the agent of the company in silence. He went home to devote the best of his years to study and experiment. Again and again his efforts were fruitless ; but he steadily answered : "There *is* a way—there *must* be one

—and I *will find it!*" Every preparation on the known earth was used in vain.

In 1835 he produced sheets of gum cloth so smooth and firm as to win him a medal at the fair of the American Institute; but he discovered, however, that a drop of acid would ruin it. The next operation, and one which, unconsciously to himself, carried him to the very edge of success, was also the result of accident.

He was one day bronzing a piece of rubber cloth, when, wishing to remove the bronze from part of it, he used aqua-fortis. This removed the bronze and in a few days the cloth had grown as hard as slate under the effects.

He produced several hundred mail bags for the government, but again the goods proved worthless. He was, however, able in 1841 to produce perfect vulcanized India-rubber with economy and certainty.

No inventor, probably, was ever so harassed, so trampled upon, so plundered by that sordid and licentious class of infringers, known in the parlance of the world as pirates, as was this man.

WILLIAM BORADORI,

1509 Kansas Street.

Polytechnic High School, Middle Class.

The above writer won the prize awarded by the Goodyear Rubber Company.

That Boy!

A LITTLE boy but ten years old
    Knew more tricks than ever were told;
    He tied tin cans to his dog's tail
And left him home to bark and wail.

His mother sighed, "*That* boy, *that* boy!
When he'll reform, I'll dance for joy;
But well I know that day won't come,
No, not until he's twenty-one.

LOUISE HOLLING.

Girls' High School, Written in Class.

5

Type.

FROM the earliest known history people have had some method of printing; at first by means of blocks cut in various designs, gradually improving until some four hundred years ago, the art of printing from movable type was discovered.

The credit of discovering this marvelous art is claimed by Lawrence Coster, between the years 1420-26, and by the Germans on behalf of Johann Gutenberg, who printed the first Bible during the years 1450-55.

The types used in printing at the present day are sorted in cases, or shallow boxes, with divisions. These are of two kinds—the upper and lower case, the latter lying nearest to the compositor.

All the capitals, large and small, accented letters, a few of the points and characters used as references, are in the upper case. All the small letters, figures, the remainder of the points and spaces to place between the words, occupy the lower case.

The compositor places his copy before him on the upper case, and, standing in front of the lower case, he holds in his left hand a little iron tray, called a composing stick. This tray is usually from six to twelve inches in length, two inches wide, and five-eighths of an inch in depth, and will hold about twenty lines of matter.

One by one the compositor lifts the letters, points or spaces into his stick, holding each one with his left hand, and placing them from left to right along the line. On reaching the end of the line, he re-arranges the spaces. When his stick is full of lines he lifts them out, and places them on a tray called a galley. When the galley is full an impression is taken of it and sent to the proof-reader, who marks upon the margin any errors he may find.

After being corrected, the matter is divided into pages of any desired size, headlines and numerals are added, the pages are secured in an iron frame or chase, the matter is again corrected, and the form is given to the pressman.

The invention of type has had a wonderful effect on civilization and commerce throughout the world. It has led to the printing of newspapers by which we are kept informed about events that happen in all parts of the world. Books have become numerous and cheap, so that education is extended to all persons.

HARRY B. GAWTHORNE,
137 Chestnut Street.

Washington Grammar School, 7th Grade.

The above writer won the prize offered by Palmer & Rey Type Foundry Company.

Carriage Manufacture.

T was a summer evening,
　The moon was up in sight ;
　We thought to take a carriage
And see the Fair that night.

My coz just from the country,
　Her name I'll tell, 'twas Kate ;
She said, " Let's see the M'chan'cal Arts,
　Although 'tis awful late."

We elbowed through the lower floor ;
　'Twas interesting there,
But Kate she said, " Just come along,"
　And dragged me up the stair.

"Now here," she said, "is what I like ;
　It just beats all the rest."
She meant the exhibition
　But said it in a jest.

For carriages and carriages
　We saw in this grand place ;
Coupés, sulkies and phaetons
　And surreys full of grace.

Cried Kate, " My eyes !　Just look at that!"
　I saw upon the floor
A cart made up in fancy style.
　I'd ne'er seen one before.

That night I dreamed that Kate and I
　In a road cart fresh and new
Went spinning 'round about the town.
　Oh !　If it would come true.

LILLIAN BRADSHAW,

2107 California Street.

Denman Grammar School, 8th Grade.

School Furniture.

IN the schools of the early period up to 1820 there was little in the way of school furniture. The blackboard was not even introduced into the city schools until about five years later, and the country schoolrooms did not have them until many years after. Globes, brought from England, were found in a few of our colleges perhaps as early as 1800, but public schools did not have them until fifty years later. Outline maps were introduced at about the same time, but were rude compared with those which we now enjoy. There was a long struggle before they were generally introduced, although now we have many sets of maps adorning our schoolroom walls.

The first school apparatus for illustrating geography, arithmetic, astronomy and geometry, by which public schools were benefited, consisted of a five or six-inch globe, a three-inch globe in halves, a few geometrical forms in wood, and a numeral frame. These were all at first imperfectly manufactured, but were afterwards greatly improved and other articles added. Competition soon brought several globes into the market at reasonable prices, and spelling-frames, large slates, chalk-rubbers, etc., followed in rapid succession, until now the furnishing of a schoolhouse costs twice or three times what the old one, furniture and all, would have required fifty years ago.

Now, of course, our schoolhouses are better built and more roomy, and also have better and more comfortable desks and seats than they used to have. In the early days of our country the school furniture was very limited. They had writing-desks next to the wall, or, rather, long boards for writing on. The benches were all loose; some of them board, with slabs from the saw-mill, standing on four legs, two at each end. Some were a little lower than the rest, but many of the smaller children had to sit all day with their legs dangling between the bench and the floor. In this respect, certainly, the children of our time are far ahead, with their individual desks of varying heights for small and large pupils, a chair, with a seat hollowed like an ordinary one, and allowing each pupil to rest his feet on the floor. Now, too, we have the benefit of good reference books that people of those days did not have, and superior globes and maps.

BLANCH DuBOIS,
313 Capp Street.

Mission Grammar School, 8th Grade.

The above writer won the prize awarded by C. F. Weber & Co.

The Advantages of a Business Education.

IN this world of infinite and varied resources and of diversified individual interests, all have something to ask, something to give and something to do. To possess the means of living, the comforts and pleasures of life, is a necessity of our existence, and this necessity or want is the basis of business.

Business or commercial transactions, as they are now extensively and intricately conducted, have developed into a science.

In any other science this would be deemed the height of folly and presumption ; yet in the science of business, which, perforce, must be every man's concern, it is tolerated and encouraged with fatal indifference to the detriment of the business world.

A beneficent government educates its children, recognizing that in their intelligence and knowledge lies its safety, progress and welfare. But at the threshold of an active participation in the serious business of a life-long struggle, the government leaves its charge with an education that has taught him naught if not the value of knowledge. It is here that a business world, supposedly alert to its every concern, shows a remarkable indifference to its own immediate and future interests by enlisting the youth into actual service without his having received any special training or education in business affairs and methods, leaving it to time and experience, the costliest of all instructors, to educate him.

The advantages of a business education are now manifestly self-evident. Educate the young man in the science of business before he enters the field of action, and, the word said, and he will advance into the fray intelligently, firmly and confidently.

In competition with his untrained co-workers, the results of a business education give him the advantage. Where they waver, he is unfaltering. What they are learning at the expense of their employers and themselves, he already knows, and his employer, daily receiving the benefits of his knowledge, speeds him on his career of progress and success.

The advantages of a business education are obviously as great as is the field in which to exercise it. It inspires us with confidence, and confidence combined with interest begets success.   SADIE GOSLINER,

236½ Eleventh Street.

Franklin Grammar School, 8th Grade.

Coal.

COAL is one of the greatest products mined from the earth. Many thousands of people work daily in the coal mines.

In early morning, in the coal districts, every road swarms with men going to the shafts of coal mines, where they are lowered into the depths of the mines, and where they work from ten to twelve hours each day. This short glimpse of daylight is all they see until they return home in the evening.

These great mines which give labor to so many people, and warmth to more than half the people of the world, are the result of some peculiar action of the earth many thousand years ago, and, although these mines are large, it is only a question of time when we shall have to fall back on our old friend, wood.

There are five fossile fuels, Anthracite, Coal, Lignite, Bituminous Shale and Bitumen. Some of these coals are much harder than others. Anthracite is very hard and takes a long time to burn, while Bituminous burns more quickly. This is due to the large amount of gas and tar oil which it contains.

All coals are composed of carbon, woody matter, hydrogen and oxygen gases; the different kind being formed by the different chemical changes occurring many thousands of years ago.

In the carboniferous ages the vegetation of the earth, which was slightly raised above the sea, was submerged and gradually became covered with sand and mud and other sediments. By upheavals of the bottom of the sea these sediments were covered with a land surface, and great masses of vegetation were formed again on top. This sunk, and in course of time was covered as before. These changes went on for ages, and in this way the stratas, in which coal is found, were formed. It was the great weight and pressure of these layers and the chemical changes which gradually mineralized this vegetation into coal.

The greatest known coal mines in the world are in England and Pennsylvania. There are large coal mines in Australia, from where they ship coal to California and other places. The most recent discovery of coal is in Nova Scotia, and is considered by many to be the largest deposit in the world.

ETHEL BECHT,

2820 Clay Street.

Denman Grammar School.

Swimming.

WIMMING, says Kingsley, should form a part of every youth's education.

Of all things acquired by the intelligence of man there is not a more beautiful or useful art than that of swimming, and among all athletic sports there is none that can in any way be compared with this in the healthful feeling and exhilaration which it produces as an after effect.

In the cultivation of swimming as an art, ten or twenty years ago, society did not take the interest, which the benefits secured through indulgence in this art merit; for bathing, of which swimming is one of the most beneficial forms, is in tropical climates absolutely necessary to the preservation of health.

Swimming is one of the most useful of all accomplishments that help to form the complete education of every gentleman. As a matter of course all other sports have their enthusiastic advocates and votaries, but of all which tend to muscular development, strengthening of the nervous system in particular, and the renovation of every function pertaining to a healthful life, swimming, it must be admitted, bears away the palm.

There is not alone this inducement to become proficient in this art, for how admirably does the noble and invigorating acquisition serve humanity in many cases of extreme peril; how many a precious life, and ships with their valuable cargoes and priceless freight of human lives, might have settled down in sight of home, and before the agonized eyes of heartbroken parents, relations or friends, but for aid of strong swimmers.

An essential part of every athletic institution of any pretension in the world, and in all places where it is possible to secure it, salt water is used, as it is considered healthier than fresh water, as the salt which constitutes part of the salt sea water has a stimulating and invigorating effect on the system; also, salt water being of greater buoyancy than fresh, is less fatiguing to swim in.

San Francisco can boast of as fine bathing establishments as can be found in the world, all of which are salt water, and no city is more fully supplied with accommodations to practice with perfect safety than our beautiful city on the Golden Gate.

IDA WATSON,
Douglass and Twenty-first Streets.

James Lick School, 8th Grade.

Written on Harbor View Baths.

Grandma's Opinion of the Sewing Machine.

YOU'VE told me, grandma, long ago,
How you women used to sew ;
And such a long time you would take
A little frock of gingham to make.

It seems to me you must have been slow,
For see how fast mamma can sew.
Oh ! tell me, then, why you were so slow ;
Could you not make the sewing machine go ?

Be quiet, child, for I must say
The sewing machine was not known in our day.
What did you do without this treasure ?
You could not of had a moment's leisure.

Oh ! tell me, then, my dear grandma,
What could be done without this guiding star ?
Then take my advice, child, when you are grown,
And have a light running machine in your home.

AGNES CORRIGAN,

2307 Mariposa Street.

Mission Grammar School, 8th Grade.

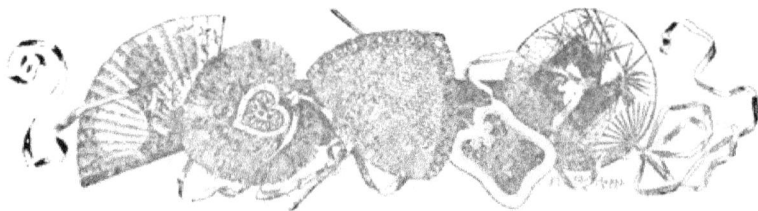

Italian Paste, Vermicelli and Macaroni.

MACARONI, vermicelli and all kinds of Italian paste are all forms of the same familiar substance much used for culinary purposes.

They are made from very white and glutinous varieties of wheat, such as are grown in Russia, Italy and California.

The wheat is ground by a peculiar process, being first wet and then heated. The flour resulting is very coarse. It is mixed with warm water and carefully worked into a uniform paste.

This paste is forced by a press through holes in an iron plate. If the holes are very small, vermicelli is thus formed. A still finer and smaller sort is called fedelini.

Large pipe-shaped cylinders of this paste constitute macaroni.

When the paste is rolled thin and cut into various shapes, Italian paste is the result. After moulding, the macaroni is partially baked.

Italy is the principal seat of this manufacture. France and England produce a considerable quantity, and of late a few firms in the United States produce an article not inferior to any of imported kinds.

OSTROILO KUCICH,

1919 Dupont Street.

Lincoln Grammar School, 8th Grade.

Why Toads Have No Tails.

WHAT a question for you to ask,
A girl in the High School middle class!
Well, nevertheless, I'll tell you how
The toad's lost the ornament of a bow-wow.

It happened that when the toad was created,
It couldn't hold still long enough to be mated ;
That is, with a tail,
So now it must wail.

JULIA EPPINGER.

Girls' High School, Written in Class.

Boots and Shoes.

CUSTOM made boots and shoes are those made to order. When the shoes are custom made they should afford the person wearing them more comfort and satisfaction than if they were already made.

A vast amount of labor is necessary before the skins of the animals are properly prepared for the making of boots and shoes.

In the tanning or tawing many men are employed filling the tannery pits, scraping, fleshing and handling the hides or skins of the cow, sheep, horse, pig, goat and even the elephant, crocodile and rhinocerous.

The art of boot and shoe manufacturing has made rapid strides during the last thirty or forty years.

The old-time shoemaker had metal patents for every size of shoes and cut uppers and soles. By these patents the uppers were "closed" together or sewed by strong waxed threads. The sewing was often done by the wife or daughter of the shoemaker. The women also bound the tops.

The shoemaker next tacked a thin inner sole to a wooden last, put the upper on a block and tacked it firmly down ; then he fastened the outer sole on with a few wooden pegs, and made a mark around the edge of the sole. It was very amusing to see him fill his mouth with pegs, which were usually of wood, take an awl in his left hand, a hammer in his right, and go to work. He make a hole in the leather with his awl, snatched a peg from his mouth, hit it a little whack with his hammer, and drove it out of sight, so that no one could see where it went.

When the pegs were all around in a neat way, he nailed some pieces of leather on for a heel. Then he filed, scraped and polished the heel and sole, and blacked and rubbed the sole and heel till they shone.

Now-a-days all the cutting, fitting, heeling and finishing are done by hand. Every operation in shoemaking is done by machinery, even the fastening of the shoebuttons.

GEORGE AHLERS,

32 Dore Street.

Franklin Grammar School, 8th Grade.

Carpets.

IN the manufacturing of carpet the weaver sits facing the loom, and fastens to each thread of the warp a bunch of colored yarn, varying in the color according to the pattern. The row being completed, he passes a linen weft through the web and drives it well up, so that all the bunches may be securely fastened. In this way narrow breadths of carpet are made, which are afterwards laid side by side and united, so as to form a large piece.

The Kidminster, or ingrain carpet, the Venetian (which was never manufactured at Venice), the Brussels and the Wilton, are some varieties of carpets in use now.

In 1839 E. Bigelow, of Boston, Mass., greatly improved the loom then in use, and afterwards by still further improvements so perfected the machinery that his loom is now wholly used.

With this loom an average of twenty-five to twenty-seven yards of ingrain carpet can be made, and from seventeen to eighteen of Brussels carpet.

He also invented a method for producing figures that would match. Mr. Richard Whytock, of Edinburgh, introduced an ingenious plan of using threads dyed of the colors in the succession they would be required. By this means a considerable proportion of the threads was dispensed with.

Brussels carpet is so named from Brussels in Belgium, whence the style was introduced into England in the last century. It is made upon a ground of linen weft, which is concealed by worsted threads which are interlaced with and cover it. The threads are commonly of five different colors. In the weaving these run the length of the web, and are so managed that all those required by the pattern are brought up together across the line of the carpet ; before they are let down a wooden instrument called a sword is passed through to hold up the threads ; this is replaced by a round wire, which, being at last removed, leaves a row of loops across the carpet. In a yard length the number of successive lifts of the sets of colors required is sometimes as many as three hundred and twenty, each of which forms a row of loops. Four colors must always lie beneath the fifth, which appears on the surface, and thus the carpet, with its linen weft, too, is thick and heavy.

Some of the most extensive carpet factories of the United States are at Lowell and Clinton, Mass., Thompsonville and Tariffville, Conn., and other cities in New York, New Jersey and Pennsylvania.

PHILIP BILL,
7 Card Alley.

North Cosmopolitan Grammar School, 8th Grade.

Chocolate and Cocoa.

CHOCOLATE and cocoa are both made from the fruit of the cacao tree, which is found chiefly on the banks of the Amazon river, South America. The generic name is derived from two Greek words, which mean God and food, and was bestowed by Linnaeus as an indication of the high appreciation in which they held the beverage prepared from the seeds.

The common tree is seldom over sixteen or eighteen feet in height. The leaves are large, smooth, glossy and elliptic, growing principally at the ends of the branches. The flowers are small and grow in clusters on the trunk and on the main branches. Generally from a cluster only a single fruit is matured. When ripe, this fruit or pod is from seven to ten inches in length, and from two to four in diameter. It has a large, thick, leathery rind of a rich purplish, yellow color, and the outside marked with eleven distinct ribs. The interior of the pod has five shells, in each of which is a row of five to ten seeds. Each fruit thus contains from twenty to forty or more seeds, which constitute the cocoa beans of commerce.

In June and December, the workmen cut down the fully ripened pods and leave them in a heap on the ground for about twenty-four hours. They are then cut open, the seeds taken out and carried to a place where they undergo a process of sweating for about two days. They are then roasted and crushed so as to separate the nibs from the shells. These nibs constitute the simplest and purest preparation in which cocoa is sold. .

Most preparations, whether sold as cocoa or chocolate, are mixtures of sugar, cinnamon and vanilla, with ground nibs; the object of the mixture being to render it easy to be dissolved in hot water. The main distinction, between cocoa and chocolate is that the former is usually sold in the form of powder and the latter is made up into cakes.

While only a small proportion of the total weight of the tea and coffee are consumed, the entire substance of the cocoa is utilized in the system. Thus while a cup of tea or coffee can be regarded as a stimulant, cocoa can, in addition, be regarded as a (stimulant) nourishing article of diet.

SUSIE M. DANIEL,

2013 Polk Street.

Spring Valley Grammar School, 6th Grade.

Reminiscences of a Gold Coin.

S long ago as I can remember I lived away down in the earth. I had many brothers and sisters, but always chose to be with a cousin of mine whose name was Silver. She was very quiet and dressed in silvery colors, while I wore golden ones.

One day the gnomes came to our home and told us that very queer things were happening on the outside of the mountain in which we lived. They said that the creatures called men were digging holes in the ground into which they were putting a black powder. The gnomes were very much frightened and said they were going to live somewhere else where they would not be disturbed. So were we frightened, but we could not go to another place as they could. We asked mother Earth what we should do, and she said to let matters take their course. Silver and I tried to imagine where the men could be going, and what they looked like.

In a short time we heard a loud blast and the side of the mountain was blown away. This scared us so that we jumped in all directions. Silver and I clung together. We were all shoveled into a sort of car and taken to a machine that was moving up and down. The men near by it were just saying that they had never found gold and silver in such quantities so near the surface of the ground. Silver and I looked at each other in surprise and wondered if the men were talking about us. We were taken out of the car and put into this machine which we heard called a stamp mill. Suddenly a man called out "ready," and we were pounded unmercifully. We felt very small as we left this terrible place.

Water was carrying us away, when we saw a friend of ours called Quicksilver. We stopped a moment to talk with him. He said if we wished he would hide us so the men could not find us for a time. We answered that we would be glad to rest, so he threw his mantle over us and we became invisible. We staid with him about a day, when a man put us all into a buckskin bag with a great many of our relations. The man began to squeeze us and Quicksilver vanished, leaving only a part of his mantle with us. It was not long after when our bag was slung over the back of a mule who carried us down the mountain to a place where we were heated so hot that we were compelled to part with the remainder of the mantle.

HELEN CLARE LILLIS,
3036 California Street.

Denman Grammar School, 8th Grade.

Grape Food.

'TIS as pure as the sparkling water,
    And is raised in the Golden State,
    Nature's own hand has procured it,
'Tis the pure juice of the grape.

For nourishment naught can surpass it,
    'Tis used as a medicine, too,
And will give the pale cheeks of the baby
    A ruddy and healthful hue.

For the tired and weary lawyer,
    Who over books does reign,
A glass of delicious Grape Juice
    Will ease his tired brain.

And for the poor consumptive,
    Whose feet totter on the grave's brink,
Some pure and sparkling Grape Food
    Will prove a nutritious drink.

And even for the physician,
    Who tries for all ills a cure to find,
A glass of Sanitas Grape Juice
    Will quiet his troubled mind.

And the clergyman, too, whose spirits are low,
    When he returns from a dire sick call,
Can refresh himself with the sweet Grape Juice,
    For it contains no alcohol.

And alas! for the wretched drunkard,
    Whose troubles never cease,
The delicious, wholesome Grape Juice
    Brings to his home joy and peace.

The Grape Juice, then, must be wholly pure,
    For on well-cultured soil it has grown,
'Tis the most nutritious beverage
    The world has ever known.

EFFIE DINNIENE,
49 Hoff Avenue.

Mission Grammar School, 7th Grade.

Grandma's Story of Jewels.

"GRANDMA, grandma, a story," cried three voices, and the little owners clambered around the old lady's knee. Grandma nodded and smiled at the bright, upturned faces and took Baby John on her lap. The other two children brought footstools and sat close by her side so as not to lose a word.

"Hundreds and hundreds of years ago," began Grandma, "long before this big, round world of ours was thought of, there lived a band of fairies, who bore the saddest of misfortunes—for the poor little things had no home. They wandered in space where nothing but darkness and confusion brooded, and even from there were they driven onwards, for the savage old King complained of their sparkle and brightness as hurting his eyes and disturbing the blackness of his realm.

"But that need not have troubled him long, for the fairies were slowly losing all the beauty which had made them seem as bright stars in a dark firmament. Just as sorrow and disappointment seemed to take the last bit of joy out of their lives and left nothing but gloom behind, a strange messenger appeared amongst them and raising its finger, spoke thus : "'Little fairies, cease weeping and rejoice, for I bring you good news. Great changes are taking place in the universe, and strange tales could I tell you, but I must hasten on. This message I leave with you : Walk directly onward until you reach an immense ball of fire—our sun—and by dancing in the rays of light, reflected on every side, you will recover your lost beauty. Here you will find a guide waiting to conduct you to the home, where your office will be to bring joy and gladness to human hearts.' So speaking, the strange figure vanished as abruptly as it had come.

"When the happy fairies reached the spot they were to call home, they danced for joy, and I do not wonder at it for it was in the beautiful land of jewels. In every precious stone crept the tiny fairies, and, indeed, much happiness have they made." Grandma looked down at the ring on her own finger and a soft moisture gathered in her eyes, for sweet visions of Grandpa and long ago came rushing back. "You see, children," she said, "as I hold my ring in the sunlight all the different colors? Well, that is nothing but the little things dancing, so happy and contented are they."

CLARA MALTER,
318 Golden Gate Avenue.

Groceries.

OF subjects great, or subjects small,
 There's one to me exceeds them all ;
 It is with us so widely known
That most choose leaving it alone.

Ah ! many forget that groceries
Are to us what honey is to bees.
As unpoetical as sugar may be,
It sweetens both our coffee and our tea.

Then there's butter, ham and eggs,
Ginger, allspice and nutmegs,
Then comes cheese, fish and flour,
All which give us strength and power.

We all like eating French Sardines,
And some are very fond of beans,
Then, if we wish pie, we must have lard,
So the crust will be neither tough nor hard.

Then come meals, both corn and oat,
And what could we do without our soap ?
Then Yankee Doodle likes macaroni,
And who refuses an anchovy ?

Many of us think puddings are nice,
But what would they be without sago or rice?
Then jelly and jam and dried fruit is fine
When for fresh fruit it is not the time.

When days are cold, soup fresh from the pot,
Made with barley or peas and with peppers hot,
Makes us forget that bad is the weather
And indoors we must stay most altogether.

Some days are short and soon comes the night,
Oil, then, must give us a light.
And oh ! how we like crackers, nicknacks and cake,
Raisins and nuts also come in first rate.

So you see, that with groceries we could not dispense,
And that this common-place subject is really immense,
That it stretches its arms the world all around,
And man cannot live beyond its bound.

So that when one writes literature, science or law,
He should not forget that groceries come before,
Giving him power his duties to do,
And to state his facts both clearly and true.

MILLIE WRIGHT,

3108 Buchanan Street.

Graduate Girls' High School.

Our Cat.

THE shades of night were falling fast,
 As o'er our back fence softly passed
 Our cat, who bore both day and night
A very sharp, keen appetite.
       Me————ow !

His voice was loud, not very sweet,
Disturbing the neighbors from their sleep,
As wildly on the night air rung
The accents of that well known tongue.
       Me————ow !

From his station on the wall
And loudly sang " After the ball ;"
And he received for his sweet tones
A shower of boots and canes and stones.
       Me————ow !

TESSIE M. DAVIDSON.

Written in Class.
Hamilton Grammar School.

JOSEPHINE FRANCIS.

The Domestic Sewing Machine.

HIGHER, higher does it climb in fame,
  Far up the mountain side of glory steep,
    That from age to age may live its name
A household word, a joy, of import deep.

Up from the countless homes far and near,
  There arises a burst of joyful praise,
From the lips of woman's happy sphere,
  For the machine that holds the *first* place.

Behold, a race for the goal it hath made,
  And won it with honors resplendent,
Lasting honors that never will fade
  While on precedence eagerly bent.

For felling, and hemming, and tucking,
  There is not a machine in the land —
Nor shirring, and braiding, and ruffling,
  That has accomplished a work so grand.

Of its lock or chain-stitch what need we speak !
There "*The Domestic*" doth surely excel.
Superlative merits it honestly reaps,
    As every one in the land can tell.

                    JOSEPHINE FRANCIS,

                        5 Guerrero Street.

Girls' High School, Graduate Class '94.

The above writer won the prize awarded by The Domestic
Sewing Machine Company.

Experiences in a Street Car.

WHEN one rides in the street cars he is sure to meet all kinds
of people, hear all styles of conversation and meet with
all sorts of accidents. You meet the person who is always fid-
geting and worrying the soul out of the poor conductor lest
he should forget to leave her off at number so and so on ——
street. Then you meet the person who is afraid he is not getting his money's worth because the car stops in the middle of
the block instead of at the corner. There is also the woman
who comes in the car with a half a dozen youngsters and has
a long argument with the conductor because he insists on her
paying one fare for every two children, while the indignant
woman strongly declares she is being robbed. Worst of all,
there is the woman who comes into the car loaded down with
bundles. She drops into the seat exhausted, and takes up the
whole bench with herself and her belongings.

How a mortal does suffer when he enters a crowded street
car, and when at last he secures a small fraction of the bench
on which he can rest his weary body, there is on one side of
him the big, fat woman who is sitting more on him than on
the seat till the poor man thinks he is going to be crushed to
jelly. On the other side of the sufferer is the man who sel-
fishly monopolizes almost half the bench and is continually
poking his neighbor as if he wants more room.

Oh, I pity the person who has to undergo these tortures.
He must surely think when he has at last reached his destination that he has repented for his sins of that day and for seven
days to come.

                    JOSIE ISAACS.

Girls' High School, Written in Class.

Bohemian Coffee.

COFFEE belongs to the medicinal class of food substances, being solely valuable for its stimulant effect on the nervous and vascular system. It increases the frequency of the pulse, lightens the sensation of fatigue, and sustains the strength under prolonged and severe muscular exertion.

The common coffee shrub or tree is an evergreen plant which, under natural conditions, grows to a height of from eight to twenty feet.

HELEN G. BARKER.

It is a native of Abyssinia and not of Arabia, for it was not known at Mecca until 1454, only thirty-eight years before the discovery of America. From Arabia it spread to Egypt and Turkey, and from Turkey was taken to England in 1650. In sixty years' time it was familiarly known, at least in fashionable society, as we find from Pope's well-known lines in the "Rape of the Sock"—

"Coffee, which makes the politician wise
And see through all things with his half-shut eyes."

It is chiefly cultivated in Arabia, the Southern States of North America, Java, Ceylon, Costa Rica, Brazil and East and West Indies; but the climate of Arabia seems more adapted to its growth.

Coffee is a powerful deodorizer; it has instantly destroyed the smell of putrifying meat; and in half a minute it has been known to permanently clear a house of the effluvium of a cesspool. To use coffee for these disinfecting purposes, dry the raw bean, pound it to a powder and roast it on a moderately heated iron plate until it is of a dark brown tint; then sprinkle it in sinks, or lay it on a plate in the room which you wish to have purified.

Coffee, as very commonly prepared by persons unacquainted with its nature, is a decoction, and is boiled for some time under the mistaken notion that the strength is not extracted unless it be boiled. But the fact is just the reverse. The fine aromatic oil which produces the flavor and strength of the coffee is dispelled and lost by boiling, and a mucilage is extracted at the same time, which also tends to make it flat and weak. The best mode to prepare coffee is to pour boiling water upon it, and set it on the fire not to exceed ten minutes. The Turks and Arabs boil their coffee, it is true, but they boil each cup by itself and only for a moment, so that the effect is much the same as that of infusion and not like that of decoction. Then again they do not separate the coffee itself from the infusion, but leave the whole in the cup.

M. Payen, by experiment, has shown that coffee is very nutritious, as it contains a large quantity of azote ; three times as much nutriment as tea and more than twice the nourishment of bouillon.

HELEN G. BARKER,

1430 Webster Street.

Girls' High School, Senior Class.

The above writer won the prize awarded by W. H. Miner.

Apostrophe to the Wind.

THOU wild and moaning Wind,
 That whistleth past my door,
What hast thou now in mind
 Of things occurred before ?

Hath Death his office filled
 In yonder lonely dell,
Where none the soil hath tilled
 Since thou a tale cans't tell ?

FLORA COLEMORE.

Girls' High School, Written in Class.

Carpets.

ADAH E. HORR.

IN early times our floors were strewn with sand, a custom still lingering in country districts ; then came the habit of spreading reeds over the floor. This use of reeds was succeeded by the employment of grass mats of simple appearance, and these by wool mats, at first chiefly imported. The wool mats were in their turn replaced by small carpets, which gradually increased in size.

Oriental carpets were first introduced into Spain by the Moors, although they had been previously used by the inhabitants of eastern countries, who threw them on the ground or floor or over the low couch on which they were in the habit of sitting or sleeping. They also added to the comfort of those who dwelt in tents, by affording warmth and protection from any dampness arising from the ground.

The use of carpets in England dates from the middle of the twelfth century, but their manufacture was not extensively carried on until the middle of the eighteenth, nearly two hundred years after it had been introduced into France and Persia by the Venetians.

Some of the best carpets take their names from the places where they were first made : Turkey carpets were first brought from Constantinople and Smyrna ; Brussels carpets from Brussels in Belgium ; and the Axminster, Kidderminster and Wilton carpets from those towns in England, although the Kidderminster carpet is not to-day manufactured in its native place, nor indeed are any of the other carpets extensively made in the towns of their origin.

In addition to the above the tapestry, velvet pile, Dutch, Venetian and printed felt are made in this country. India and Turkey carpets are imported, and imitations of them are made in the United States, principally in Philadelphia.

The reproduction of the old patterns have been taken from the paintings of the old masters.

In some paintings by these artists may be found carpets copied with such wonderful minuteness of detail, that the very stitches of the pattern may be counted. But the Venetian painters, whose opportunities were the greatest, were so negligent in their attention to detail that it is impossible to obtain a single perfect pattern from the whole of their productions.

The selection of carpets for a house is of the utmost importance, and should dominate the rest of the furniture and hangings.

ADAH E. HORR,

2207 Webster Street.

Pacific Heights Grammar School, 7th Grade.

The above writer won the prize awarded by Joseph Fredericks & Company.

Apostrophe to a Mosquito.

OH ! thou instrument of torture,
   With all thy implements of pain,
   Which affect us like a scorcher
And nearly drive us all insane.

Why did'st thou leave thy early home
Far down in stagnant water deep ?
Why on our land beloved roam
And baffle all attempts to sleep ?

ADRIA L. SHAW.

Girls' High School, Written in Class.

Italian Paste, Vermicelli and Macaroni.

ITALIAN Paste is made from wheat flour. The wheat after being well washed is ground to a flour. It is then sifted about five times, the last being sifted very fine, and the flour that is produced is used. Hot water is then added until the flour becomes a paste.

This paste is called Italian Paste, and is used to manufacture Macaroni and Vermicelli.

Macaroni is manufactured from a dough called Italian Paste, made from wheat flour. After this

ERNEST COTTER.

dough is made it is kneaded by placing it into a wide cylinder, opening and rolling over it a heavy stone wheel, and thus pressing into wide sheets of dough.

It is then cut into pieces by the workmen and placed into a large cylinder perforated. The dough is then forced out of the cylinder by a heavy pressing of a press coming through the cylinder. During this process the Macaroni is partly baked by a fire near the cylinder. As the Macaroni comes out it is cut off into desired lengths by the workmen.

The Macaroni is then placed away or hung up for a few days, and is then ready for use. Macaroni is generally colored yellow. This is made by the use of saffron and eggs.

Macaroni was invented in Italy, and is made there more than in any other country. Imported Italian Macaroni was considered the best in the United States, but the Macaroni manufacturers in this country now produce as good Macaroni as the imported.

Macaroni when it is to be shipped or exported is put into boxes in about twenty-five pounds to the box. The box is made air-tight by covering the edges of the box with colored paper. Put up this way it may be kept a long time in any kind of climate.

The ordinary way Macaroni is cooked is this : The Macaroni is put into boiling hot water and cooked until it becomes swollen and elastic. The water is then poured off and a gravy which is prepared from some beef is then poured over it. This is the quickest and the cheapest way to cook it.

Vermicelli is made nearly the same way as Macaroni. Instead of being pressed through large holes it is put through very small ones, making them fine and hair-like. This is the only variation it has from the Macaroni process.

ERNEST COTTER,

522 Sixth Street.

Franklin Grammar School, 8th Grade.

The above writer won the prize awarded by C. R. Splivalo & Company.

The Moon.

OH, thou fair ruler of the night.
   May my prayer ascend to thee.
   Send down thy silvery light —
A blessing on my boy at sea.

His ship is on the ocean wild,
   He thinks perchance of home and me.
In God's own image bless my child,
   And guide my boy at sea.

It may be many years before
   That ship returns again, and we
Know that in that distant shore
   Thou wilt love my boy at sea.

EMILY R. COEY.

Girls' High School, Written in Class.

THE ADVANTAGES OF A BUSINESS EDUCATION.

ALICE M. JOHNSON.

A BUSINESS education is of advantage to the rich, the poor, the young, the old, and the woman as well as the man.

One is taught by a thorough business training to be accurate, concise, p u n c t u a l a n d thoughtful.

We all know that to a poor boy an education in drawing or music would probably be u s e l e s s, while a thorough training in arithmetic, pen-m a n s h i p, correspond-ence, etc., would enable that same boy to enter an office and soon work his way up in the world.

For a boy whose parents possess means it is especially essential that he be carefully instructed to take care of the property his father has accumulated, and how proud that father is who, in his declining years, can shift the great burden upon his young son and feel sure his hard spent energy has not been in vain.

On the other hand, we will picture the boy whose business education has been neglected. He is careless, lazy, unable to add or write. Such a young man, if thrown upon the world, must take a very inferior position and there remain.

Enough of the boys, for I desire to relate the glorious advantage of a practical education for girls. Many people think girls should never know anything but sewing, housekeeping and such employment, but my opinion is that young ladies should have an opportunity to do as well as the boys.

I knew a family in well-to-do circumstances with two daughters who had been given lessons in all fine accomplishments, but neither one could add correctly. They thought it very tiresome to learn such bothersome things as sewing and cooking, for they would always be rich and never need to work.

The time soon came, however, that they regretted having spent their time so idly, for their poor father died suddenly and left his estate so entangled that they could hardly get bread enough. The unfortunate girls felt terribly to see their poor mother live in such want, so they determined to swallow their pride and go to work, but then the question, ''What shall we do?'' arose before them like a cloud.

After trying in vain to get work, without knowledge, they set about to procure the needed business education, and after very diligent study the eldest young lady secured a position as stenographer in a large firm, while her sister keeps books for another corporation.

They now are able to live comfortably, and their only regret is that they had not learned earlier in life to care for themselves in any emergency that might arise.

I have endeavored to show how very necessary a business education is to all, and I advise every girl or boy never to consider themselves fully educated until they hold a certificate showing a complete knowledge of the rudiments of business life.

ALICE M. JOHNSON,

2517 Fillmore Street.

Pacific Heights School, 6th Grade.

The above writer won the prize awarded by Heald's Business College.

"THE DAISY."

LITTLE daisy in the field,
    Peeping upward toward the sky,
Trying thy gentle head to shield
    From cruel feet that pass thee by.

We will not pluck thee, gentle flower,
    We will not mar thy beauty rare,
Rest through many a sunny hour,
    Blest by God as his flower fair.

NETTIE ROTH.

Girls' High School, Written in Class.

Millinery.

REBECCA HESS.

IN taking up the subject of Millinery, the first thing to consider is the origin of the word. We find that Milan, at one time, was renowned for the elegance and tastefulness of its finery, and became so noted as a leader of fashions in Europe, that the English word milliner originated from Milaner, an importer of fashionable articles from Milan.

As the season is summer, and it is the time for straw hats, I shall begin by telling about them. Some seeds were dropped down into the earth and soon some grasses sprouted up. The stems of these grasses were dried, and made into straw, and the straw was braided. Then these braids were sewed together by the Bosworth straw-sewing machine, which is used almost entirely in the United States. The hat is next pressed by another machine which is of American invention, which smooths it ready for trimming. Four hats can be pressed by this machine in a minute.

Although we now have the straw hats, and if it were necessary would be able to wear them as they are, still they are not complete. Trimming is needed. Ribbon is most commonly used for trimming. The silk fibres are obtained from the cocoons. A number of these fibres are taken and slightly twisted, and put together so as to form a thread called a single. These threads are then spun or woven into a ribbon, which for hats is generally from three to five inches.

Flowers are also important in trimming hats, which are, of course, artificial. Some are made of silk and others of velvet. The stems are made of green cloth or wax.

Now that we have the shape, the ribbon and the flowers, the question is what should be done with them.

The very first thing to do after we have the straw is to line the hat. The lining is usually of a fine, thin silk and is procured in much the same way as ribbon.

Now the difficult part comes. The difference between a hat trimmed by a French milliner and that trimmed by a novice is much the same as the difference between a butterfly, which is airy and graceful and beautiful, and a crab, which is very awkward but still useful. We will suppose this hat to be turned up at the back. Then the ribbon is taken and put around the sides of the hat, and at the front a bow is made in such a way that there will be two loops on each side, and in the center will probably be a buckle made of brass. Then a bunch of the flowers are taken and arranged in some graceful manner, perhaps coming up from the back part of the hat. A few flowers coming down from the hat and falling on the hair would add to its beauty.

REBECCA HESS,

1800 Sutter Street.

Denman Grammar School, 8th Grade.

The above writer won the first Prize awarded by The " Wonder " Millinery Company.

What a Hat!

WHAT a hat that woman in the car did wear !
Why, it was the very color of her hair ;
Just as red as the reddest brick,
With a feather in the side as stiff as a stick.

But I suppose the owner thought it very fine,
While to me it looked as if but a dime
Had been spent upon this tasty (?) purchase
And as if the trimming might have once been a kerchief.

Perhaps she had saved that very stiff feather
(Probably it and the other trimming together)
From her Great Grandmother's old collection,
But think her taste n'er ran in that direction.

FLORENCE NIGHTINGALE.

Girls' High School, Written in Class.

Millinery.

COLORS should be chosen, not because they are fashionable, but for the reason that they are becoming, otherwise ill effects will be the result. To face a hat or bonnet you should sew the wire all around, about one-fourth of an inch from the edge of the brim ; then fit the velvet or satin on the brim, by pinning it on the wire, turn in the edge of the material and slip-stitch it on ; if you want to put on a binding instead of a facing you must sew the wire

HELEN FRENCH.

on the edge of the hat or bonnet. For shirring take one-half yard of satin or silk, cut on the bias, divide it in two equal parts, join the parts together, turn in one of the edges and put in a row of shirring, allowing just enough space to put in the wire ; then add as many rows of shirring as you need. To make a frame smaller remove your wire, cut off what you please and replace the wire as before.

A hat may be trimmed with lace, ribbon, beads, feathers, flowers, satin, velvet or veiling. Beads look well either with flowers or feathers, but generally feathers are used on a hat with beads. Gros-grain and ottoman ribbons are more fashionable than satin, nevertheless the latter are still worn, and look pretty, and are cheaper than silk. Beads are not worn on hats as in former years. For deep mourning crape only is used, and the bonnet must be made perfectly plain. If a bonnet is too small in the head, sew a piece of buckram on the edge, and then sew the wire over the buckram. To make a stylish bow of ribbon, take one and one-half yards of ribbon, draw it in tight folds, then twist the thread around tight, make as many loops as you have ribbon without cutting it, put a knot in the middle, and arrange your loops so as to lay flat on the hat. When a hat is large after facing it, you can use one or two large plumes. For shirring use either silk, satin, velvet or lace. A great many people object to wearing crape, but a plain silk bonnet may be worn.

A stylish bonnet for a middle-aged lady is made by trimming it on one side with a long plume, and on the other side by a handsome bow of ribbon or a knot of velvet or satin. Another way is to take velvet cut on the bias, catch it in the middle in a tight knot, sew it on the brim of the bonnet previously bound, then draw the velvet on each side of the bonnet in soft folds, so as to make it puffy; it forms a large bow and is very neat.

Many people have an idea that they are capable of imitating a hat or a bonnet by merely asking the price, and observing the manner in which the artist has designed it; but when the imitation appears on Kearny street the difference is remarkable. Ladies cannot expect to make, without experience, what it has taken years to learn in business life. And for this reason I would suggest that what you spend for " ice cream " you give to the milliner, so that you do not look like a home-made girl.

HELEN FRENCH,

330 Duncan Street.

James Lick Grammar School, 5th Grade.

The above writer won the Second Prize awarded by The " Wonder " Millinery Co.

The Brook.

OH, Brook! Thou flowest on and on,
    Through meadow, wood and lane;
Thou babblest still from morn till dawn,
    Thou know'st not mortal pain.

Over the rocks and shrubs you go,
    Though having ne'er a thought;
And murmuring in tones so low
    Of pleasures you have brought.

FRANCYS ROSENSTIRN.

Girls' High School, Written in Class.

Out-Door Sports.

TROUT-FISHING.

FRANK METTMAN.

I SPENT my last three summer vacations in Los Gatos, Santa Clara County, California, where I had a good chance for trout-fishing, which is my favorite out-door sport.

While there I went fishing most every day, and the creeks I fished in were the Los Gatos, the Guadaloupe and a creek that flows through Congress Springs and Saratoga, all of which are good trout streams.

The time I found best for fishing was from five to nine o'clock in the morning, and in the evening from five o'clock until dark.

A split bamboo pole is best for trout-fishing, but possessing none, I used a common limber bamboo pole, a sea-grass line, a cat-gut leader, and fly-hooks numbering from nine to twelve.

I also used ordinary trout hooks, and baited them with garden worms or periwinkles.

Some people do not know anything about periwinkles, but the trout like them very much and will eagerly go for them.

The periwinkle is a kind of a worm found in the bed of the creek. It lives in a cylinder-shaped case which it makes of wood, gravel and other hard substances; this case is about an inch long, a quarter of an inch thick, and looks like a small piece of wood.

Trout always swim up stream towards the head-waters; they are great jumpers, and I have seen them jump up a waterfall four to five feet high.　　　　FRANK METTMAN,

915 Twentieth Street.

Horace Mann Grammar School, 6th Grade.

The above writer won the prize awarded by Clabrough, Golcher & Company.

THE REASON.

OH dear, the pies are not browned,
   And I've spoilt the apple sauce ;
I havn't put the roast in yet,
And everyone is cross.

The kitchen is just filled with smoke
   And the fire won't burn at all.
The oven isn't the least bit hot,
   And I'm sure the cake will fall.

'Tis all on account of this terrible coal,
   For it burns like a piece of stone ;
And I promised Sue I'd go out with her,
   But now I guess she'll go alone.

And here comes Mrs. Rogers ;
   Such a neat person as she
When she sees this untidy kitchen
   Will have her opinion of me.

But when Mrs. Rogers entered
   And saw the sorry plight,
She introduced the Wellington Coal
   And set the matter right.

The girl in long years after
   Thought of the dear old soul
And the days of peace and comfort
   Since she used the Wellington Coal.

EFFIE DINNIENE,

49 Hoff Avenue.

Mission Grammar School, 7th Grade.

7

Jewelry.

TO improve our personal charms jewelry has been resorted to as far back as memory reaches, and, no doubt, it began with the very first of the human race. In ancient times people had to be contented with leaves, flowers and branches of trees.

Those living on the seashore were fortunate to add shells of many colors and hues, arranging them in the shape of necklaces, bracelets and so forth. Even birds had to be robbed and killed, so that people could ornament themselves with their plumage.

Gold and silver are the most precious of metals that are used in jewelry. Gold can be beaten twelve hundred times thinner than printing paper. Both gold and silver are too soft to be used alone in jewelry, so they are alloyed with other metals.

Silver is the second precious metal. It is of a whitish color; it is soft, but not as soft as gold. Silver is seldom found in its pure state ; it is generally mixed with gold. It is ductile and also malleable like gold. Silver is found in Arizona, California and Germany. Silver is obtained like gold, by grinding and sieving it ; then quicksilver is put with it, and then heat is applied ; after the quicksilver goes off as vapor, the silver is left pure. Silver is used a great deal by chemists and dentists.

Gold is used in jewelry in many different ways ; for instance, in rings, bracelets, pins, penholders, pens, earrings, medals and many others.

The following stones are only a small number of what is used by the jeweler : The diamond, the ruby, the emerald, the opal, amethyst, topaz, agate, bloodstone, moonstone and the pearl.

The diamond is the hardest of all stones, and used to cut all the others. In very few places they are found near the surface of the earth. Diamonds, on account of their scarcity and brightness, are the most valuable of all stones used in jewelry. Their value is estimated by carats. Diamond fields are found in Brazil, Australia, Siberia and India. South Africa is also celebrated on account of its valuable diamond fields.

GEORGIE A. HARRIS,

615 Bush Street.

Denman Grammar School, 8th Grade.

Swimming.

SWIMMING is an art ; as it comes natural to beasts, should be practiced by man. No race of mankind can be mentioned to which swimming is unknown, and in many barbarous countries it is more common than among the civilized nations.

Salt water is best to learn swimming in, as it is more buoyant than fresh.

Confidence in one's self is one of the essential points in swimming. All artificial aids such as corks, air-belts, etc., should not be used, for they lift the body too high out of the water. The simplest and plainest stroke in swimming is the breast stroke. The stroke is executed by lying with the back upwards, and placing the hands on the breast with the palms downward, then pushing the arms forward to their full extent, after which the palms of both hands are turned outward, and making a stroke with both hands to the right and left through an angle of 90°, and carrying the hands back to the starting position. During the motion of the arms the legs make a similar motion. The movement of the arms keeps you floating, and the movement of the legs pushes you forward.

Another mode of swimming is by the over-hand and side stroke. The quickest and easiest stroke is the over-hand stroke ; one good stroke carries the swimmer six feet in two seconds.

A good swimmer is known by the way he enters the water. A dive when properly performed is a very graceful feat to the eye. A dive is executed by keeping the feet and legs together, bending slightly toward the water, and then swinging the hands above the head. All the power possible must be used by the legs in jumping off the board. When in mid-air the body is straightened out. The descent is made by bending the arms downwards and entering the water fingers first.

LEO LEBENBAUM,

1522 O'Farrell Street.

South Cosmopolitan Grammar School, 8th Grade.

The above writer won the second Prize awarded by the Olympic Salt Water Co.

Pure Paints.

PAINTS are formed by mixing colored powders, called pigments, with oil, water or other fluids.

Knowing what paints are, we now have the task before us to find from what sources they are obtained. Perhaps this is one of the most interesting of experiments, and annually there is found some new material from which colored material or pigment is made. If we look into this subject we will find that native-colored earths is one of the essential compositions from which paint or colored material is manufactured. Secondly in importance we see metallic compounds, and last, but not least, other mineral resources. These are the three principal things from which the first process of making paint is obtained.

The one peculiarity of paint, and one of its principal characteristics, is its power of fully covering any surface on which it is spread. Of course this is dependent upon the qualities, and in view of this fact it should be applied and spread uniformly, and, if it then dries quickly by natural heat, it is then said to be of a quality commendable to use.

When dry it should resist change of weather to which it is exposed, and to be a high grade, first-class article, it must possess a certain degree of brightness and tinting power, and when mixed with other colors should not be injurious either to its own color or to the color that it is mixed with.

Paint is so varied that it is necessarily a fact that its uses are also varied. It can be a chemical, a crome material or ultramarine. Paint for houses is made by a process of grinding and mixing, that is, simply the raw material ground to a powder and then soaked in oil or some other fluid.

Artists' material is much different, it being a great deal finer and possessing more tint. These pigments or powders are mixed with very fine liquids, and we have the beautiful tint from which our great artists have painted the pictures by which they became famous. In this connection it may be said that some paints are made from substances known only to their makers.

The principal pigments may be classified and described as follows : White lead, zinc and antimony ; blue (not extensive), ultramarine, Persian blue, indigo, yellow-ochres, gombage and tints.

Red has an inorganic origin, and contains oxide of copper. Green contains hydrate oxide of copper, magnate of baryte and oxalt of cobalt.

We have now given an account of paints, their use, composition and origin, let us now in conclusion say that they are the promoters of that grand and divine oil called "painting." Where would ancient Rome and Greece be were it not for these bits of colored material ?

Paints are the preservers and originators of great art, and by their use we are enabled to gaze upon grand paintings, landscapes and pictures which otherwise would have been hidden from " Modern Civilization."

ROSIE CAHEN,

1044 Golden Gate Avenue.

South Cosmopolitan Grammar School, 7th Grade.

What Are the South Winds Saying ?

WHAT are the south winds saying
　　As they wander lazily by,
　　And what do they tell to the treetops
　Which makes them bow to the sky ?

Why are they not in a hurry
　Like the bustling winds from the North,
And why do they play round the garden
　And call all the little weeds forth ?

MAMIE BARRETT,

Girls' High School, Written in Class.

The Land Where the Lost Things Go.

FAR away in fairy-land seas,
　　With shining wings spread to the breeze,
　　Fairies bring queer things to and fro
To a little isle where the lost things go.

Whenever a plaything, large or small,
Is left in the yard or left in the hall,
These little nymphs with laughter gay
Come with wings swift and convey it away.

GRACE SELLON.

Girls' High School, Written in Class.

Type.

TYPE consists of raised letters or characters, cast in metal or raised in wood, and are used in printing. Although the knowledge of how it is made can be easily obtained, there are many that know little about its manufacture. Some printers or compositors who have used type nearly all their lives know little about its manufacture, or even what it is made of. In the following I shall endeavor to tell you what I have learned of its manufacture : Type is made of a composition of metals which generally consists of lead, tin, antimony and copper. The first step in the manufacture of type is the cutting of the letter desired on the end of a piece of hardened steel. This piece of steel is carefully shaped to the proper size, as it must be perfect.

By means of this punch, as it is called, an indenture is made in a piece of copper, which is afterwards shaped and polished, and is called the " matrix." In this indenture in the matrix the face of the type or letter is formed. The rest of the type or body is formed in what is called the " mold," which is made of hardened steel. The " matrix" and "mold " are combined and constitute the moulding part of the type-casting machine which manufactures type at the rate of from one hundred to one hundred and seventy-five per minute. The modern type-casting machines finish the type and are generally used. When the old style machines are used the type is finished by hand in the following manner : First, there is attached to each a wedge-shaped piece of metal, which has to be broken off. This piece of metal, however, has to be on the type when they are cast in order to have them the required length. In breaking off this piece of metal there is a roughness caused, which, after the sides are finished, is removed by planing a groove in the body of the type. The type is now finished, and, after the defective types are picked out, it is packed and sent to the purchaser, or laid away to await orders. The importance and necessity of good type is very great, as good printing cannot be done with imperfect type. Although some type is used in the manufacture of rubber stamps, the largest portion is used in printing. A great deal of type is used in making what is called a stereotype, which facilitates the printing of large newspapers, etc. Type is not sold by the piece, as many would suppose, but by the pound. Movable metal type were first used in printing in the latter half of the fifteenth century.

J. GILBERT RECHEL.,

1003 Valencia Street.

Mission Grammar School, 8th Grade.

Man's Inhumanity to Man.

SINCE the world was created, and since Adam tried to throw the blame of his disobedience on Eve's shoulders, the wheel of "Time" has been going steadily round, watching the decay of nations and the destruction of noble cities and towns.

It has never paused in its course, and has beheld the advancement of man, as his narrow ideas have changed or broadened, and his knowledge of the unseen wonders of Nature become expanded.

But one thing has not changed (the feelings that predominated in man in those early days, still hold sway over him.

Cain slew Abel, and to-day numberless men are branded as Cain was. Above all the mean petty feelings of pride, jealousy and spite, the one great sin of cruelty and inhumanity reigns.

It is impossible to conceive how one man gifted with talent, wealth and strength, can look mercilessly down on his less fortunate brother, and bid him work for his daily bread.

The rich man turns the beggar from his door, hungry and unsatisfied, and yet he goes to church and kneeling reverently, says : "Give us this day our daily bread."

Man, the all gifted, with his strength of mind and body and his right to rule over the earth, is often little better than the brute.

We all know the story of the "Fox Without a Tail." All through life we meet with many tailless foxes, who not content with their own degradation, desire to drag others down with them.

These undesirable animals constantly appear before us, with their friendly advice. We must beware of them or we will find that they are leading us down their own dark pathway, away from the light of honesty and truth.

Thus the inhumanity of one man to his brother fills the world with sorrow and misery, for we are all brothers and sisters, and the earth is our universal mother.

Our earthly fathers as well as our Heavenly One, look with sorrow on the work of their sons, for :

> ￪ Man's inhumanity to man,
> Makes countless thousands mourn."

FRANKIE SULLIVAN.

Girl's High School, Written in Class.

Photography.

APPARATUS.

IN photography certain apparatus or tools are needed to produce a picture ; some must be bought, others with but little ingenuity and labor can be made.

The first essentials are the camera, the lens, the plate-holder, the tripod, the cloth and the focusing-glass.

The tripod is the stand on which the camera is placed : it can be taken apart and when not used can be folded and carried in the hand. The extension tripod has particular advantages, as it can be made to stand on uneven ground, so that the camera may be brought to a proper level by simply adjusting the legs.

The cloth must be about one yard square, of a dark quality and impenetrable to light.

EXPOSURE.

Exposures in the exterior should be shortest, 11 A. M. to 2 P. M. No attempts should be made to work on objects when a fog obscures the distance to the eye. The camera and lens must be free from dust ; holders must be tightly closed before leaving dark room.

The tripod must be set firmly ; the focus, with a large stop in lens, on an object say one hundred feet away ; fix the sliding front, and turn the camera each way till the subject is on the ground glass.

Remove ground glass, take plate-holder from box and put it in front of ground glass; draw the slide with steady motion entirely out with a quick motion. You are now ready to expose.

Uncap, give time and recap.

Return slide you have removed.

DEVELOPING.

Chemicals needed to compound developer :

Sulphite of soda, crystal..........................1 pound
Carbonate of potash, granulated.... ....1 pound
Carbonate of soda, granulated....................1 pound
Pyrogallic acid...................................4 ounces
Sulphuric acid.... ....1 ounce
Bromide of potash................................1 ounce

This quantity of chemical furnishes enough developer for

almost three hundred plates 6½x8½, and, if carefully used, not cost more than one cent for each.

To compound the developer, do as follows :

Procure two twelve-ounce bottles of clear, white glass, with well-fitting corks. Mark one "No. 1, Pyro.;" the next "No. 2, Potash." Take eight ounce graduate, put five ounces water; add two ounces sulphite of soda crystals and stir with glass rod till it dissolves; then slowly add half a dram, fluid measure, of sulphuric acid; add two hundred and forty grains pyrogallic acid; when dissolved, fill up to eight ounces. The details of the making of the developer cannot be entered into too closely. We will say the developer is done.

Lay the plate in tray, face up, and pour the developer over it.

A darkening appearance gradually grows distinct in a few minutes. These are the sky, high-lights, or light objects on which has fallen most powerful light.

To examine its intensity, hold it to the light, and if not intense enough continue these operations till it is. The negatives are washed in chemicals and water, and dried on a negative drying-rack.

It is next varnished by a very simple process. The paper for it is prepared, and after going through several other processes the photograph is finished.

CHARLIE THALL,
1124½ Folsom Street.

Franklin Grammar School, 6th Grade.

The Wind.

OH wind ! Oh wind ! thy mighty blast
   Hath o'er the sea such doom o'ercast ;
And Oh ! how many a mighty sail
Hath floundered in tempestuous gale.

And oft hath left fair silven strand
From some far distant smiling land ;
And many a maid and mother weep
For a loved one, lost in surging deep.

GRACE M. COLE.

Girls' High School, Written in Class.

The Sewing Machine.

THE superior merits and the attractive beauty of the sewing machine demonstrate the fact that it is one of the greatest marvels of the present century.

If we would learn of the intrinsic value of the machine, or become acquainted with the grand record of the sewing machine in general, we must take a retrospect of a period in which there has been toils and triumphs. If, in order to do this, we traverse the bridge of history, which spans the gulf of time, we find revealed to us an array of facts which prove conclusively that our own epoch, when compared with those which have preceded it, is pre-eminently an age in which difficulties have been met and overcome by noble efforts and marvelous skill.

In the domain of mechanical art the steam engine occupies a very high place, and, if it is appropriate to regard it as king of machines, then the proud position of queen of mechanical contrivances is possessed by the sewing machine. Her throne is within the domestic circle ; her reign has been prosperous and happy. By a wave of her sceptre she has driven tedious labor from the mansions of the wealthy, and banished from the homes of the poor that drudgery, weariness and sorrow which is so graphically described by Thomas Hood in his pathetic poem. Since he wrote the ''Song of the Shirt '' the merry voice of the sewing machine has been heard amidst scenes of gladness, comfort and ease.

Many names have been identified with the sewing machine, but it remained for American genius and inventiveness to produce a machine fit for practical use. This was affected step by step.

It has always been the aim of the sewing machine manufacturer to produce a superior article. The machines are made of the very best materials. All the wearing parts are accurately gauged ; skilled inspectors scrutinize every part before being put together.

It is made up in mahogany, maple, walnut, oak and olive. In design it is very beautiful ; its relative proportions are pleasing to the eye, and, to all who possess it, it will be a '' thing of beauty and a joy forever.''

JEANIE LINDSAY,

406 California Avenue.

Columbia Grammar School, 8th Grade.

SCHOOL FURNITURE.

SCHOOL furniture is an index of civilization. The absence of fine furnishing in a modern schoolroom is a sure " tell-tale " that the Trustees of that district are lacking in refinement. They unconsciously advertise themselves as having been taught in some country school, where long benches without backs served as seats, and a painted board on "legs" served for a blackboard ; and an apple and knitting-needle, borrowed from one of the girls, served to illustrate " the earth on its axis." And even that unpleasant aspect of the case is not its worst. As the lack of refining influences at home make rough boys and rude girls, so desks and seats that do not inspire the scholars with neatness and tidiness are a positive injury. Environment is considered by many to be a great factor in making or marring character, and what environment can work more mightier than school life ?

Seats made in artistic finish and with an understanding of the form of the human body ought to be compulsory in every schoolroom ; otherwise, physical injury results to the children. Seats also ought to be selected from the best made, as the pupils' eyesight and form depends largely on them. A poorly made desk is often accountable for the drooping shoulders and hollow chests we see among school children.

Mr. Ruskin tells us that he was made an artist and an art critic by his father never permitting him to see anything rude, rough or inartistic. What an inducement this, for our fathers to make our schools as near a refined parlor as possible ! It will pay them, and it will cause us in after years to rise and call them blessed. The maps and globes ought to be of the best and truest that genius has produced. Just here some one may complain of the cost of all this. Well, even the cost is not so much as one would think, for the difference in price between a good article and a cheap poor one is nothing when divided up among a lot of people ; and when we consider how much longer a good article wears, I think it pays to buy a good one.

There is really no excuse, and none ought to be taken, for bad furnishings in a schoolroom at the close of the Nineteenth Century.

JOHN COLBERT,

634 Elizabeth Street.

Lincoln Grammar School, 7th Grade.

MILLINERY.

THE art of trimming headgear is called millinery. The making of hats or the foundation upon which milliners work belongs to a different branch of business. Millinery gives an agreeable and pleasant occupation to thousands of ladies of our land. However, all who undertake the trade do not make a success of it, because they have not the knack of planning so that the colors will blend, and arranging their work to suit the complexion and style of the wearer. Thus, we see the art must not only be acquired, but one must have a natural taste for it if she expects to make a success of it.

After the work has been arranged by pinning the material in place, no particular skill is required to do the necessary stitching, but it is in arranging the material that the natural talent is required. Then, too, in millinery the style is the principal thing to be considered. Therefore, those who make a business of the trade must keep themselves well informed on the latest colors, styles, etc.

Not long ago a party was given by one of the young ladies of a small town, and each lady invited was to bring with her an old straw hat (that was past using for anything else), a lot of ribbons or decorative materials, a needle and thread. These furnishings were to be given to the young men present, and they had the task of trimming the different hats, without any assistance, as best they could. A prize was to be given to the gentleman who trimmed the hat or bonnet best, and a booby prize was to be given to the one who was least successful. You can imagine how artistically and gracefully they started to work, some displaying their beautiful diamonds which were seldom noticed by the ladies, while others struggled with a piece of thread that had in some way become entangled in the artificial flower they were attempting to put on. At last, after struggling with the flowers, hat and ribbon for a whole hour, the young ladies took pity on their various efforts, and they were allowed to discontinue their work. It was quite laughable to observe the colors and the arrangement on some of the hats ; and I am quite sure the young lady who had to wear any of this beautiful millinery would say many disagreeable things about the trimmer.

This illustration is made for the purpose of showing the necessity of undertaking only such things as we are most capable of performing.

GRACE BERRY,
515 Jones Street.

Denman Grammar School, 8th Grade.

NOTHING

WHEN asked to choose a subject
    For an essay yesterday,
Among a thousand topics
    I roamed for hours away.

I could not write upon the moon,
    Nor on a daisy fair,
Nor on the dear mosquito
    Whose music fills the air.

And so I asked my teacher
    If she could help me out
She said, "Why write on nothing, *that's*
    What *you* know most about."

And so I write on nothing.
    What is it anyway?
It's what I have inside my head
    And what I learn *all day*.

           BESSIE BALDWIN BEARDSLEY,
Written in Class.

Which?

IF in the course of our short life
    Some task unpleasant be our lot,
Shall we rebel—bemoan our fate—
    Then turn our back and do it not?
Or shall we check our great dislike,
    At once perform it with a will
That robs the labor of its sting,
    And turns to good the fancied ill?

           AGNES O'CONNELL.
Girls' High School, Written in Class.

WELLINGTON COAL.

WELLINGTON coal is mined on Vancouver Island in British Columbia, from where most of it is exported to San Francisco.

The many excellent properties of this coal are well known by nearly every one. There are few who believe in burning cheaper-priced coal, which burns fast and gives little or no heat; makes a great quantity of ashes, and clogs the flues with soot ; and if a lid of the stove is lifted, a great quantity of smoke issues forth and fills the room and very often the whole house.

Wellington coal has none of these faults. It is a clear and steady burner, making very little smoke and hardly any soot, and never fills up the ash pit near as fast as any of the cheaper and inferior brands do. It is also a coal that may be termed a long burner, as it does not need replenishing as often as the others do, but keeps a long steady fire, giving plenty of heat and requiring none of the attention the others do.

It is not only a good cooking coal, but its good burning qualities are innumerable. It makes an excellent grate fire, and it can be utilized for almost any purpose where a good burning coal is required.

Wellington is a coal that has few equals, if any, among bituminous coal, and is always uniform in quality. The price is nearly always the same reasonable figure, making it within the reach of every one. The many good qualities of this coal point to it as a coal superior to all ; it is in almost every usage to which coal can be put, and maintaining that it is always best and the cheapest money can buy.

MARION HENNESSY,

1505 Clay Street.

Denman Grammar School, 8th Grade.

Inflamed with the study of learning and the admiration of virtue ; stirred up with high hopes of living to be brave men and worthy patriots, dear to God and famous to all ages.

—MILTON.

Education is the only interest worthy the deep, controlling anxiety of the thoughtful man.

—WENDELL PHILLIPS.

DRUGS.

OW, uncle, please do listen,
　　I must write a composition on drugs.
Oh, dear! It's a difficult subject.
　I would much prefer writing on bugs.

" But still, it must be written,
　And er— Oh, uncle! Can you not see
I compose so very poorly,
　You must write this composition for me."

Ruth's uncle was a great tease,
　So he said, " Very well, I will write
So simply that all will think, dear,
　'Twas done by yourself, pretty sprite."

He sat at the table and scribbled
　For a half a minute or more,
Then Ruth slyly looked o'er his shoulder
　And this is what the child saw :　　.

Extractum Colocyntlidis Alcholicum,
　Extractum Camabis Purification,
Extractum Colclici Aceticum,
　Extractum Serpentariæ Fluidum.

She was thoroughly disappointed
　When these Latin words met her eye,
Tears in her brown eyes glittered
　And she looked quite ready to cry.

But her uncle turned and said,
　" More highly I value truth
Than all the learned essays
　That were ever written, Ruth.

"A falsehood you would be acting
  If you handed my essay in ;
Though you wouldn't mean to be untruthful,
  Falsehood is a deadly sin."

So Ruth sat down and thought,
  Into the evening far,
Till the night drew down her curtains blue
  And pinned them with a star.

When the silver huntress, Diana,
  Through the window ventured to peep,
The essay now was all written,
  The composer fast asleep.

On a chair by the open window
  A small, white paper lay ;
On it was carefully written
  That memorable essay.

The virgin moon dropped lower
  And bent her dainty head,
And glancing o'er the paper,
  This is what she read :

In the golden days of long ago,
  When through the heavens wide,
Apollo and the huntress queen
  Wandered side by side,

No drugs were known to ancient men
  And so the people died,
And never knew that drugs would save
  Them from the rushing tide.

'Twas left for modern men to know
  The science God has given
To relieve pain and sickness cure—
  'Tis a gift direct from heaven.

Opium, morphine and cocaine,
  And drugs well known to-day,
We've heard of chloroform effects on men,
  And physicians often say,

Perhaps 'twere well for many men
  That these drugs ne'er had been known,
For though they are truly remarkable,
  They have ruined many a home.

When Ruth awoke in the morning,
  Great was her surprise,
For the paper was wet as though with tears,
  Shed by sorrowful eyes.

MOLLIE SULLIVAN,

625 Natoma Street.

Clement Grammar School, 8th Grade.

A Poem.

OH, would that I could write a poem
    To make the world wonder and stare,
    To make souls soar to heavenly things,
  Away from this strife and care.

It would make the sorrowful happy,
  The children laugh in their play,
The old and the feeble feel young,
  And the sick and oppressed gay.

But what is the use of telling
  What I could never do ;
Perhaps 'tis best to do God's work
  And be upright, honest and true.

To be happy each day as I can be,
  And make others happy, too ;
Not simply to talk of helping,
  But be willing to work and do.

God judges the gift by the giver
  In the Book of Truth, we are told ;
And He prized the widow's mite far more
  Than the nobleman's broad piece of gold.

MAY NUTTING.

Girls' High School, Written in Class.

8

Statuary.

IN the fourth century A. D., under the rule of Constantine's successors, sculpturing was in v o g u e, though the productions were not of a high order. The old Pagan faith of the Romans was dead, and they had not been as yet sufficiently influenced by Christianity as to embody their belief in their work. Is it not n a t u r a l if a sculptor has a n y noble ideas of worship that he will bring them out in his statues? Therefore, when these are lacking, the result is dull and lifeless. Gradually great improvements were made by Christian workmen, proving that the higher the ideal, the greater the work.

BLANCHE LEWIS.

Among the Grecian sculptors Phidias stands out pre-eminent. He was born about 500 B. C. His first two important works were executed in bronze. The first was a large group dedicated to Delphi ; the second a colossal statue of Pallas Athena. But the two works with which his fame is chiefly associated were in gold and ivory—the colossal statue of Athena, which is at the temple dedicated to her, and the other of Jupiter, for the temple at Olympia. The god was represented as seated on a throne, his right hand holding a figure of Victory, and his left resting on a sceptre, on which the eagle was perched. On his head was a wreath of olives. The drapery was of gold, richly worked with flowers. The throne was mostly of ebony and ivory. Of this, the greatest work of the greatest Grecian sculptor, nothing but the description remains. A great number of Phidias' pupils also arrived at great distinction.

Among the later Italian sculptors we find Michael Angelo,

the greatest and most famous of the celebrated artists of Florence, born in 1475.

His first essay in sculpture was an aged fawn with a front tooth knocked out.

One of his statues, which he produced in 1495, called "St. John in the Wilderness," is at present in the Berlin Museum. The stripling saint stands naked but for a skin about his loins, holding a honeycomb in his left hand, and lifting to his mouth with his right a goat's horn full of honey.

One of the most prominent at the World's Fair was the one of Columbus represented on the deck of the Santa Maria. On the top of the pedestal at his feet is the vessel's anchor, and in his hand is a pair of dividers, as though he had just picked out his course on a map. The face of the great "Admiral" is more satisfactory than in most of his portraits.

Another statue that attracted my attention was that of Cleopatra. It was one of the most graceful and symmetrical pieces of art seen at the Great Fair. She has often been used by poets as well as by sculptors to represent their ideals of loveliness.

BLANCHE LEWIS,

1420 Sutter Street

Denman Grammar School, 8th Grade.

The Brook.

WINDING down from the mountain top
Comes the crystal stream,
Bubbling, gurgling, refusing to stop,
As in a happy dream.

Finally it reaches the dark blue bay
Where it must ever be,
Until on some eventful day
It finally reaches the sea.

MARGARET MAGUIRE.

Girls' High School, Written in Class.

Arabian Coffee.

COFFEE is the seed of an evergreen shrub, the *Coffea Arabica*, which is said to have been discovered in Abyssinia by the Arabs. It is chiefly cultivated in Arabia, the Southern States of North America, the East and West Indies, Java and Ceylon; but the climate of Arabia, where it was first cultivated, appears to be most suited to its growth. Frequent rains and the brilliant unshaded light of the almost cloudless sky stimulate vegetation and cause the secretion of

ESSIE BAUM.

those principles on which depend the delicate aroma. Elevated situations are most suitable for the growth of coffee, and the plantations have much the appearance of pleasure grounds. The trees are raised from slips which are allowed four or five years to grow before they are cropped. They attain the height of eight or ten feet, and continue in bearing from thirty to fifty years. The shrub or tree resembles a handsome laurel, and bears a profusion of clusters of fragrant white flowers, which are succeeded by brilliant red berries, sweet and pulpy, which ripen to a purple color—each containing two coffee seeds or stones. The process of preparing coffee for market is as follows: The ripe berries when picked are at first put through a machine called the despulpador, which removes the pulp; the coffee grains are still covered with a sort of glutinous substance which adheres to the bean; they are now spread out on large "patios," made specially for this purpose, and left there, being occasionally tossed about and turned over with wooden shovels until they are perfectly dry. They are then gathered up and put into the "retrilla," a circular trough in which a heavy wooden wheel, shod with steel, is made to revolve so as to thoroughly break the husk without crushing the bean. The chaff is separated from the grain by means of a fanning mill and the coffee is now thoroughly dry and clean. After this, it is the custom of some planters to have it spread out on long tables and carefully picked over by the women or children, all the bad beans being thrown out. It only remains then to have it put into bags, weighed and marked before it is ready for shipment to the port. On some of the larger plantations this process is greatly simplified with considerable saving in time and labor by the use of improved machinery for drying and cleaning coffee.

ESSIE BAUM,
2918 Jackson Street.

Pacific Heights Grammar School, 7th Grade.

The above writer won the First Prize awarded by Hills Brothers.

The Daisy.

O H ! you pretty daisy,
    What a lovely flower ;
Wafting perfume o'er the earth,
    And gladdening every hour.

Peeping through the moistened soil,
    When trees and fields are bare ;
And, though tread on by many feet,
    The daisy is still there."

HILDA LEVY.

Girls' High School, Written in Class.

Arabian Coffee.

THE Coffee tree is a native of Eastern Africa, but it was in Arabia that it first became known to the people of Europe, and until about the year 1700 A. D. that country afforded the entire supply.

The coffee seeds then found their way to Java by some traders, and one of the first plants grown on that island was sent to the Governor of the Dutch East India Company, who lived in Holland, as a present. It was planted in the Botanical Gardens at Amsterdam, and in a few years seeds were taken from it and sent to South America, where the cultivation of coffee has steadily increased, extending to the West Indies, until now the offspring of this one plant produce more coffee than is obtained from all the other plants in the world.

The plant is an evergreen, and is from six to twelve feet high, and the stem is from ten to fifteen inches in diameter.

When the blossom falls off, there grows in its place a small green fruit, which becomes dark red as it ripens.

This fruit is not unlike the cherry, and is very good to eat. Under the pulp of the cherry is found the bean or berry that we call coffee, wrapped in a fine thin skin. The berry is at first very soft, and has a bad taste ; but as the cherry ripens the berry grows harder, and the dried-up fruit becomes a shell or pod of a deep brown color. When the berry is ripe it is of a translucent green color.

The coffee tree begins to bear fruit the third year, and by the sixth or seventh year they are at full bearing, and continue to bear for twenty years or more.

LULU A. WEGENER.

Before the berry can be used it undergoes a process of roasting. The amount of aromatic oil brought out in roasting has much to do with the value of coffee when it is sold, and the longer the raw coffee is kept the richer it becomes in this peculiar oil, and so the more valuable.

Arabia produces the celebrated Mocha coffee, which is the finest in the world. Java coffee is next prized.

LULU A. WEGENER,
1421 McAllister Street.

Hamilton Grammar School, 7th Grade.

The above writer won the Second Prize awarded by Hills Brothers.

The Language of Flowers.

I STOOD in a beautiful garden,
   Where the flowers reared their heads,
To tell me their significance,
   And this is what they said :

The white rose, ''I am worthy of you,''
   The red one, '' Love me ever,''
Next the yellow oped her lips and said,
   '' Do not let us sever.''

The violet blue, '' I am ever faithful,''
   The snow-drop, '' I have hope,''
The little daisy next did say,
   '' No one can with you cope.''

And each to me did breathe some tale
   Of what they do express ;
Some told of love, of joy, of faith,
   And others of distress.

MARTHA TRIEST.

Girls' High School, Written in Class.

Benefits of the Installment Plan.

THE installment plan means to pay down a given or named sum, and thereafter pay small payments until the debt is covered.

A young man is just started out in life (for instance) and he works hard for his salary, which is not very large. With this money he has to pay his room, his board and buy wearing apparel. After his working hours are over he does not wish to appear in his working clothes, but wants a good, stylish wearing suit, and, as he has not enough money to pay for a suit at once, he is in a fix how to obtain one without paying all down. At this moment he falls to the Installment Plan and sees the clear future before him of owning a fine suit by paying a certain sum down and paying a payment every week. He makes arrangements for the suit which he receives, and before long the money is all paid up.

Another person, a lady, has a drunkard for a husband who brings home very little money for her to support her children and herself with. As she is a neat and honest woman, she wishes to put herself and children in better attire. Maybe she came from a better family and has quite a number of friends who often come to see her. Of course she does not want to be embarrassed by her friends because her parlor is not carpeted or she has not nice chairs in it. She saves as much money as possible and goes to an installment company and paying this money down receives the carpet and chairs and pays the balance in weekly payments. When her friends come to see her again they are greatly surprised, and she feels

WALLACE W. WIDEMAN.

in her heart a feeling which only a discoverer or conqueror feels when he conquers or discovers a new piece of land.

Another benefit: A married man has a wife and children, and, as he sometimes stays out later at night than he should without his really meaning to, he catches it from his wife when he comes home that night. So he says to himself, "I must buy a watch some way as my staying out at night arouses ill feeling in the family, and I want a good watch, but that costs too much money for me to pay down at once. Well, yesterday I heard that the installment company has some fine gold watches and very cheap," and so saying goes to the installment house, examines the watches and finds them to be of the finest workmanship and fine time-keepers. He picks out a watch, pays the first payment down, which exceeds the rest, and finishes up by weekly or monthly installments, as the case might be agreed upon.

WALLACE W. WIDEMAN,
2515½ Bryant Avenue.

Boys' High School.

The above writer won the prize awarded by The United States Watch and Suit Co.

Only a Minute.

HOW many when at work or play
And called by parents dear away,
Turn back and say with nothing in it,
"All right; I'll be there in a minute."

How much can happen in that time!
Something great in history's line,
Something by which to be made known,
Something on which we stand alone.

Then list to parents, children all,
Be sure you heed, then, every call;
And do not say with nothing in it,
"All right; I'll be there in a minute."

NELLIE MITCHKUS.

Girls' High School, Written in Class.

Hardware.

LILLIE FRITSCHL.

THE subject of hardware is such a vast one if you choose to enter upon it as it deserves. There would first have to be considered the production of raw material, then the manufacturing of the same into merchantable goods.

When we look into the tastefully arranged windows in which the goods of the different hardware stores are on exhibition we realize the fact that these same articles must have been subjected to the skill and ingenuity of many different kinds of workmen.

We all know that iron is the main factor in the manufacturing of hardware. It is obtained through mining. Iron mines are to be found in this country, on the Atlantic Coast and also to some extent in the upper Mississippi Valley. Iron mines are worked by shafts, which are sunk into the ground, and from which tunnels are dug, called levels. As fast as the ore is hauled to the shaft it is hoisted by means of machinery to the surface, where it is loaded into cars and hauled to the crushers. These crushers are very large, ponderous machines, which break the ore into suitable size, being then separated from its drosser elements, and delivered at the furnace where it is moulded into bars.

It is from these bars that hardware is manufactured. They are taken to the factories and by means of machinery are made into such articles as hammers, files, planes, locks, keys, wrenches and innumerable other things.

Hardware enters into the use of everyday life to such an extent now that we cannot imagine how people could have gotten along without it. What was a luxury a hundred years ago is now a necessity. For instance, how could the primitive way of erecting houses, without the use of hammer and nails, satisfy the enterprising builder of to-day?

As we superintend the construction of a modern house hardware is required in many ways. We must have locks and hinges for doors, springs for windows, casters for beds, bureaus, tables and other articles of furniture, which without those useful contrivances would be too heavy to move.

Could we manufacture furniture without the use of tools? Must we not have planes to smooth the boards of our tables from which we eat our food? Could a tree be felled without the use of saw and axe? In fact, there is not a single article of furniture used which could be made without one instrument or the other.

As we enter the kitchen one of the most important articles used in house-keeping is the stove. Must we not have pots, kettles, frying pans and other kitchen utensils to prepare our food? The thrifty housewife would be perplexed indeed should she have to get along without the flat-iron.

As already stated, hardware enters not alone into the manufacturing of articles absolutely necessary, but also into those of games and all kinds of athletic sports.

LILLIE FRITSCHI,
613 Bush Street.

South Cosmopolitan Grammar School, 8th Grade.

The above writer won the First Prize awarded by the Osborn Hardware and Tool Company.

The Moon.

OH moon! that art so high and bright,
  What meanest thou by thy good light,
And why appearest thou so sad
  When all the people seem so glad?

Why smilest thou not like thy friends
  Who try kind looks to thee to send?
And if thou doest as I say
  Thy face will beam like light of day.

EMMA KOCH.

Girls' High School, Written in Class.

Hardware.

F we look into a hardware store we shall see flat-irons, knives, razors, nails, screws, scissors, carpenters' tools, hatchets and other things too numerous to mention, all made of iron and steel. Even the steel is made of iron, so that about everything in a hardware store is turned out of the iron mines. Thus you see the value of iron. It is much more useful than gold or silver, and, in fact, almost every other kind of metal.

ARTHUR COUSINS.

Hardware is one of the most valuable productions of iron. What would we do without knives, razors and, most of all, our nails, screws and tools? for by those things we build our houses and stores. How would the carpenter get along without his hammer to drive the nails with? The head of the hammer must be made of iron, for lead or wood would not do, for they would easily break, and the lead would easily bend and get full of nicks.

Iron is hard and will stand a great deal. What would we do without any axe to split our kindling with? We could make an axe out of nothing but iron. If we examine the edge of an axe we will see that it is highly tempered to make it hard and durable. The blade of our pocket knife is made of iron and goes through a process until it becomes hardened ; then through another process which gives it a high polish ; it is then called steel.

The cheaper a knife is, the more like iron the blade is. A razor is much better tempered than a knife. The ladies' and tailors' tool is the scissors. It is very useful to them. We couldn't very well do without them, for all our clothing and a great many other things are cut out with them.

All these things come under hardware, so one can see its value. Hardware is a general name for all wares made of iron or other metals, as pots, kettles, saws, knives, etc. A hardware-man is a man who sells all these things. Hardware is in every household, and is the product of the iron mines. Hardware ranks from the smallest tack to the largest cooking utensil. A vast amount of iron is used in hardware, so that there must be many mines in the world to supply all the hardware stores.

ARTHUR COUSINS,
200½ Ninth Street.

Franklin Grammar School, 6th Grade.

The above writer won the second prize awarded by the Osborn Hardware and Tool Company.

The Prettiest Room I Ever Saw.

OF all the pretty little rooms,
The prettiest of them all
Is the quaint old-fashioned library,
That is just across the hall.

Its hangings are deep crimson,
Its chairs are just the same,
But they are all of leather
Excepting the wooden frame.

The books upon the wooden shelf
Are the finest of their kind,
For they contain some knowledge
That has rare excelled its time.

The quaint old-fashioned fireplace,
The lighthouse of the room,
Makes all things look so happy
And takes away the gloom.

MAUD ITSELL.

Girls' High School, Written in Class.

Rubber Goods.

FREDDA COOL.

RUBBER is used extensively both in the arts and sciences, being light and a non-conductor, and in its free state very flexible and a non-absorbent.

It is put to various uses. Some of the most familiar are water-proof clothing and covers, tires for bicycles, packings for machinery, hose for fire departments, innumerable and beautiful toys for children, and thin sheets called rubber dam, which is used principally by dentists.

It was discovered by Charles Goodyear of New Haven, Connecticut, that by mixing sulphur with rubber and submitting it to a high temperature it became very hard and admitted of a fine finish ; in this condition it is called vulcanite. It took a great deal of experimenting to attain this result.

In this form some of the most important uses are a base for artificial teeth, ear-trumpets, eye-glasses and combs, etc.

Rubber in its primitive state is collected very like maple sugar, being the sap of a tree and gathered with great patience and labor.

After the tree has been discovered an incision is made, and the sap is allowed to run into vessels of various shapes and sizes.

In former times rubber was known as elastic gum, but received the name of India rubber from the discovery of its use in rubbing out black lead marks, for which purpose it was first imported, being much valued by artists and sold at a high price.

It is obtained in considerable quantities from South America, British India, the poorest kind coming from the western coast of Africa ; this rubber is clammy and offensive in odor and only slightly elastic.

Denman Grammar School, 8th Grade.

FREDDA COOL.
22 Kearny Street.

What the South Wind Tells.

THE sultry, balmy day was done,
  Soft breezes gently stirred the air,
  The new-born stars looked down on one
Who stood within a garden fair.

White blossoms of the orange tree,
  Their soothing fragance 'round her shed,
And as she looked out o'er the sea,
  All gladness from her heart had fled.

Still as she gazed, from out the west
  A gently gliding boat appeared.
As yet she could but see the crest,
  Her heart beat faster as it neared.

Within the gondola she spied
  The form of one for whom she yearned,
He pushing onward with the tide,
  His vessel to her quickly turned.

From off the orange tree above
  She plucked one tender blossom fair,
While in her eyes there shown a love
  Beautiful in its sad despair.

Upon the dainty little flower
  She pressed a long and fervent kiss,
She knew that he must go this hour —
  The lover that had brought such bliss.

She threw the bud into his boat,
  He took it with a hopeless sigh,
For on the fragrant flow'r she wrote
  Her farewell. And he glided by.

Still from the south the faint breeze blows
  Amid the orange blossoms white.
It is the wind alone that knows
  Of the parting one sad night.

KATHRYN GAINES.

Girls' High School, Written in Class.

A Sewing Machine—Autobiography.

I AM a machine of the first class, that is, I am obedient, useful and obliging. I never get cross when my mistress is in a hurry to finish a dress for a ball or party, nor do I let any of my most important parts get out of order, but I try to do my duty and keep up my good name.

I am handsome, as well as useful, and help to make the sewing room look bright and cheerful. My sides are smooth and bright, and the fancy trimmings about me glitter as the sun looks in through the open windows.

IRENE MACDONALD.

I was made from a lofty tree which grew in a large forest. I spent many happy days of my childhood with my companions, and many a friendly chat did we have. But when we grew older our troubles began.

One day some men came and cut us down. We were then sent to the mill where we were cut and planed, and made into different shapes.

Next we were sent to the factory where our different parts were put together, and fancy fixings of iron were put on us. Soon we were completed and were surprised to see such a lovely lot of things.

After our stay in the factory we were sent to a storeroom ; while we were there we heard that we were to be sent to the World's Fair. We had heard the workmen in the factory talking about this place and were very glad to get a chance to go there.

We had to travel about a day before reaching the Fair, and when we arrived there we were placed in a large building. It looked very pretty to see so many machines and such pretty

ones, and many a lady stopped and looked at us and said:
"Don't I wish I had one of those."

We remained in the World's Fair until it closed. Then we
were boxed up and we knew that we must be going on another journey. We had brought a great deal of honor to our
owner in the World's Fair, and for this reason we were to be
sent to the California Mid-Winter International Exposition.

When we reached the Mid-Winter Fair building we were
put in a large room. Here we staid until the Fair closed.
Many ladies stopped and looked at us, but one lady I noticed
in particular stood and gazed at me for a long time.

When the Fair closed we were offered for sale and that very
lady bought me and took me home and placed me in the sewing room. When any of her friends called on her she would
take them into the room where I was and say: "See my new
machine. Isn't it a beauty?"

IRENE MacDONALD,

435 Fifteenth Street.

Mission Grammar School, 8th Grade.

The River.

IN the heart of the snow-capped mountains, far from all
    haunts of men,
Where the fierce and hungry panther howls in his lonely den,
A spring with waters clear and cold, with low and tinkling
        sound,
Had bubbled up so joyously from the sterile, rocky ground.

O spring, thou little knowest the sorrow thou shalt see
When a broad and mighty river thy waters have grown to be.
Past fields and towns and hovels and groves of willow and
        leech,
Till the great and noisy city thy waters at length shall reach.
And oh! the want and suffering thou then shalt look upon,
And many a soul sick and distressed
Find freedom from care on thy breast.

FLORENCE BOSTON.

Girls' High School, Written in Class.

9

Sporting Goods.

O far as we know, there were very few ancient games in which artificial implements were essential. In some sports the quoit or discus, a heavy circular piece of metal or stone, was thrown as a trial of strength.

In boxing the hands and arms were covered with thongs of leather, called cestus, designed for protection to the wearer, as well as means of annoyance to his opponent. The cestus were sometimes loaded with metal, and serious injuries were often inflicted.

R. H. KELLEY.

Note the difference between this present age and the era just spoken of. In this century and country more attention is paid to the gun and fishing tackle than any other form of sporting goods, although the football, baseball, etc., and gymnasium are very popular.

All guns not designed for military purposes are classed as "sporting arms." Great improvements have been made in these, one of which is the rifled over the smooth bore. Rifles are measured by a small instrument resembling a carpenter's compass, called a "caliber," which shows the exact size of the bore, and from it we get our term forty-two "caliber." Rifles carry from one hundred to fifteen hundred yards, and are used principally for heavy game and target shooting. The standard American rifles are the Winchester and the Marlin. One of the latest Winchesters is a repeating take-down rifle. It is made in various calibers. The magazine is so constructed that it unscrews and the gun can be taken apart and packed in a guncase like a shotgun.

Shotguns are made in eight, ten, twelve, sixteen and twenty gauge. Hammerless shotguns are much preferred to the old style, the hammers are invisible, and the gun is cocked by a small catch or button placed either on the top or on the side of the stock, just in the rear of the triggers. In a few fine guns the discharged cartridge is thrown from the chamber by an automatic ejector when the gun is opened. The repeating shotgun carries six shells in a magazine like a rifle, and is manipulated like one as well.

As angling becomes more popular, more fishing tackle is used. The finest trout poles are made of split bamboo, weighing from four to ten ounces; they are very flexible and strong. The best lines are made of silk, oiled or prepared by a process to make them water-proof. Trout and salmon flies are made so skillfully as to deceive the most wary fish; multiple reels and reels that wind up the line automatically.

Football, baseball and lawn-tennis goods are used a great deal, and who knows but all the healthy out-door recreations in which the sporting goods of this country are used may develope a much healthier, stronger race of people than are inhabiting the United States at present?

R. H. KELLEY,
1505 Jones Street.

Spring Valley Grammar School, 8th Grade.

The above writer won the First Prize awarded by E. T. Allen Company.

Ocean Depths.

ROLL on, old ocean, roll, thy billows high I see;
   Now, as in days of old, for mine I look to thee,

Yes, many years have passed since on that summer morn
Her fair form went to thee and left me here forlorn.

But some day from thy depths in joy her soul shall rise,
And meet mine far above, beyond the deep blue skies.

HELEN BOYLE.

Girls' High School, Written in Class.

Sporting Goods.

REBECCA ELLINGSWORTH.

OUTDOOR sports are rapidly becoming popular, or, in fact, they are v e r y popular already. Ladies give a great deal of attention to them now-a-days, whereas in former years they sat at home in their parlors and were afraid to be strong and healthy, but wanted to a p p e a r weak and delicate; while now they are all in the tennis-c o u r t or on t h e beach, etc. Men too give a great deal of attention to outdoor sports. B a s e b a l l, football, tennis, cricket, etc., are all very popular sports.

In all our colleges and universities all the sports are kept in practice, and the young men and women show how much good it does them by their strong muscles, rosy cheeks, good broad chests and stout, healthy limbs.

Fishing, yachting and hunting are all enjoyable pastimes or sports. In every sport is to be found some benefits as well as pleasure. If the people keep up this fashion which has become so beneficial to their health, the future generation will be a large, strong, healthy race, and an honor to their country, for with healthy bodies come good thoughts and healthy minds. When a person is well we know that he can think and work far better than if he were weak and sickly. So I think that all these great things will come from good, healthy outdoor sports.

Fishing is an old sport, but it is one that becomes more popular from year to year, especially among the wealthy class. A great deal of pleasure is to be derived from fishing, and ladies are taking a great deal of interest in it, as well as many other sports.

Yachting is a very enjoyable sport, and it is very healthy, because the fresh breeze from the bay or ocean invigorates the body.

Lawn-tennis is the English national sport, but the people of America are rapidly adopting it as their favorite. Baseball seems to be the most popular among the men and boys. Cricket is also a sport which is played more in England than in America. Golf is a game which is but little known in America, but in England and Scotland it is played quite frequently. It is hoped that it will be introduced into American society and sporting clubs before long, as it is a game which has many pleasures for both old and young. Croquet is also a very popular sport, but is enjoyed more by young people.

REBECCA ELLINGSWORTH,

509 Leavenworth Street.

Denman Grammar School, 8th Grade.

The above writer won the Second Prize awarded by E. T. Allen Company.

Only a Minute.

WHEN husband and wife are off for the ball
And he for his wife is compelled oft to call,
All of a sudden he hears from the hall
"Only a Minute!"

But he, you must know, is not often severe,
So he tries hard to be of good cheer;
He waited for her what did not appear
"Only a Minute!"

MAY LIPPITT.

Were I an Artist.

WERE I an artist I surely would paint,
Taking my brush in my hand,
A beautiful girl with a face like a saint,
In form and in feature so bland.

She should be fair as the bright morning sun,
Her hair as gold as its rays;
She should be equaled scarcely by one
Who lived in those good old days.

MAY LIPPITT.

Girls' High School, Written in Class.

Gold and Silver Refining.

GOLD when taken from the mines always has some silver with it, and often other metals. Silver does not always contain gold.

Refining is done in several ways. I shall speak of but two. In some refining works silver is separated from gold by sulphuric acid, but in the mint usually by nitric acid.

There is no acid that alone can dissolve gold, but this is not the case with silver. The process of separating gold from silver by sulphuric acid is as follows : they are united in the proportion of not less than 3 parts silver to 1 of gold and melted together. Sometimes more silver has to be added than at others, for the amount contained in gold when it comes from mines varies from 3 to 30 or 40 per cent. After they are melted they are put into iron pots containing sulphuric acid, and heated. The sulphuric acid separates the silver from the gold, and the gold falls to the bottom as a brown powder. The contents of the iron pots are then subjected to hydraulic pressure and the water is squeezed out. The gold is gathered and melted into bars which usually contain from 992 to 999 thousandths of gold, the rest being silver.

The solution containing the silver is drawn off into large tanks or vats, in which are hung copper plates. Chemical action takes place which separates the silver from the sulphuric acid and the silver falls to the bottom in metallic form. All of the solution except the silver is forced out by hydraulic pressure. The silver is then melted into solid bars. The bars generally contain from 997½ to 999½ thousandths of silver ; the balance is copper.

HELEN CLARE LILLIS.

In the process of refining with nitric acid the gold and silver are mixed, and melted as in the preceding method, but are refined in porcelain jars instead of iron pots. Nitric acid instead of sulphuric acid is used. The nitric acid separates the silver from the gold and the gold falls to the bottom. The gold is separated from the solution by hydraulic pressure, gathered and melted into bars as when sulphuric acid is used.

Common salt is then added to the solution containing the silver, and chemical action takes place.

The silver is thrown to the bottom as chloride. This chloride is treated with metallic zinc, and the result of the combination is metallic silver which is dried by being squeezed in the hydraulic press. After being melted it is made into bars having about the same degree of fineness as when treated with sulphuric acid ; that is, $997\frac{1}{2}$ to $999\frac{1}{2}$ thousandths of pure silver, the rest being copper.

Gold refined in these ways is worth about $21.6718 per ounce, and silver is worth about 65 cents—the present market price per ounce, but at par formerly was $1.2929 per ounce.

HELEN CLARE LILLIS,

3036 California Street.

Denman Grammar School, 8th Grade.

The above writer won the First Prize awarded by The Selby Smelting and Lead Company.

What a Daisy Told.

BEAUTIFUL, starry blossom, emblem of innocence,
White as the fallen snowflake, pure as an angel's kiss,
Unrivaled you bloom in the meadow, happy, gay and content,
Loved and caressed by the sunbeam, till he sinks to sleep in the west.

Sought by the fair-haired city belle, sparkling, lovely and sweet ;
Oh, after leaving her lover, how she longs your face to greet,
To search the dreamy future, to repeat the old rhyme o'er —
Does he love me, little flower? unfold your secret, I implore.

And there in the golden sunlight, in the meadow's broad expanse,
She removes your snowy petals, the last one falls—she laughs,
And turning, smiling brightly, skips lightly o'er the ground,
Locked in her girlish bosom, the secret she has found.

ETHEL I. KENNEDY.

Girls' High School, Written in Class.

GOLD AND SILVER REFINING.

Y adding three parts of silver and one of gold you make an alloy that can be separated by the sulphuric acid process. The silver will go into solution, leaving the gold at the bottom of the boiling pot ; the silver is then syphoned into a large tank, leaving the gold in readiness for melting. This process is usually adopted for separating, etc., the gold from the silver on a large scale. It appears to have been proposed in France by Dize at the beginning of the

MABEL SANDERSON.

present century. It was actually in use in France in 1820, and was introduced into the Mint refinery at London by Mr. Mathison in 1829. It is based upon the facts that hot sulphuric acid converts silver and copper into soluble sulphates without attacking the gold, the sulphate of silver being subsequently reduced to the metallic state by copper plates with the formation of sulphate of copper.

When the acid has ceased to act on the metals, a small quantity of sulphuric acid of a specific gravity is added, and after a second boiling the contents of the vessel are allowed to settle.

Silver extraction is very easily effected by means of the process of cupellation, one of the oldest metallurgical operations which dates back to a time beyond that of Pliny. The metal is placed on a shallow kind of a dish made of compressed bone-ash powder, and the whole forming a reverberatory furnace, and therein kept at a red heat in the presence of an abundant supply of air.

The lead is oxidized in litharge, which at the temperature prevailing melts into a thin liquid, and is made to go off through a slit or hole made in the side of the "cupel" or "test;" the silver remains unchanged, so that the regulus becomes richer and richer as the process proceeds. The foreign base metals, as will readily be understood, go off as oxides along with the first portion of the litharge, and accordingly can be removed without contaminating the bulk of the latter product. When the percentage of the silver increases to about eight per cent., the regulus as a rule is transferred to a fresh cupel, and thereon treated in the same way as before, until the last trace of litharge is seen to go off as a thin film on the regulus, presenting, on account of its thinness, in the glow of the fire the magnificent appearance of a soap bubble in sunlight.

The silver then is "fine," that is, almost pure; it is then refined with acid. As a rule this silver contains more or less gold, and the gold must be taken from the silver before it is ready for the market.

MABEL SANDERSON,
821 Jessie Street.

Clement Grammar School, 8th Grade.

The above writer won the Second Prize awarded by the Selby Smelting & Lead Company.

THE LAST CAT.

'TIS the last cat of the cellar,
  Left meowing all alone,
All his furry companions
  Are drowned, dead and gone.
No puss of his kindred,
  No Thomas's in view
To join in serenading
  And give mew for mew.

I'll not leave thee, lone feline,
  To pine on the fence,
Alone to encounter
  Mighty missiles intense.
So kindly I offer
  This old sack instead.
Come, go where thy brethren
  Lie senseless and dead.

ELSIE KRAFFT.

Girls' High School, Written in Class.

Statuary.

STATUES are made of marble, plaster of paris and bronze. In fact, nearly all metals are used for statuary.

The most beautiful and most expensive statues are made of Carrara marble, which is found in the mountains and hills around the city of Carrara in Italy.

Two of the most noted and most beautiful statues are those of Venus and Nydia the blind girl. Venus was the Roman goddess of love, and was so beautiful that many sculptors have taken her as a model. Nydia was also a beautiful girl who lived in Pompeii.

JOSEPHINE LIPPINCOTT HOFMANN.

The museums of Italy are filled with beautiful relics of Greek statuary.

At Paris are the noted statues of Venus, Diana, the Gladiator and Archilles.

At Sutro Heights are many beautiful statues. It is very kind of Mr. Sutro to make such a beautiful place for the public and to try to interest the people of San Francisco in statuary.

In Golden Gate Park are many beautiful statues, but not as many as at Sutro Heights, and I hope in years to come that many more statues will be placed in the park.

At the Midwinter Fair there were a few beautiful statues of Carrara marble in the Liberal Arts building, and also some in the Fine Arts building. The statue of Queen Isabella, made of plaster of paris or gypsum, was also very beautiful. It represented her offering to pawn her jewels if there was not enough money in the treasury for the outfit for Columbus.

The sculptor has to have a model of clay, plaster of paris or some other substance before he can commence his statue of marble.

Bishop Doan has shown us in these lines how like sculptors
we are and how we can make our souls into beautiful statues :

" Chisel in hand stood a sculptor boy,
  With his marble block before him,
And his face lit up with a smile of joy
  As an angel dream passed o'er him.
He carved that dream on the shapeless stone,
  With many a sharp incision,
With heaven's own light the sculpture shown,
  He had caught that angel vision.

Sculptors of life are we as we stand
  With our souls uncarved before us,
Waiting the hour when at God's command
  Our life dream shall pass o'er us.
If we carve it then on the yielding stone
  With many a sharp incision,
Its heavenly beauty shall be our own,
  Our lives that angel vision."

                    JOSEPHINE LIPPINCOTT HOFMANN,
                                    1219 Bush Street.

Denman Grammar School, 8th Grade.

The Song the Winds are Singing.

WHAT is the song the winds are singing,
    Those mournful sounds—what do they tell,
Do they sing of sorrow and sadness,
    The hearts of men to swell ?
Do they sing of the vices of mankind
    In that song so dull and drear—or
Are they messages from foreign lands,
    Those mournful notes they bear ?

                              FRANCES JUDSON.

Girls' High School, Written in Class.

The Ocean.

O THOU wild and stormy ocean,
    Who but bends the knee to thee ?
Man must e'er show his devotion
    While his ships sail on the sea.
Thou carest little for iron or wood,
    And in thy wild tempest wrath
Devoureth ships as man his food
    Leaving no trace of their downward path.

                              MAE MELROSE.

Written in Class.

Pure Paint.

THE word paint is a name which is generally applied to mixtures of soluble colors or pigment, or colors with certain materials, to prepare them for application to surfaces such as wood, iron, stone, plaster, etc., with the aid of a brush.

Paints are used not only for the purpose of decoration, but to protect surfaces from moisture and decay. All paints consist of two parts, namely : the pigment and vehicle.

JAS. McDERMOTT.

The pigments are varied in character ; the whites are generally white lead, more or less adulterated, barytes, oxide of zinc and prepared chalk. The yellow color is made up of chromonate of lead, etc.

The reds are made up of vermilion, lead, etc., which nearly all other paints are made from. The most common vehicles of oil paints is linseed oil, which is very valuable because of the property that it possesses ; that is, it holds the paint in a firm, waterproof sort of varnish.

For many purposes paints are prepared with the aid of water as a vehicle, glue and gum being added to make the pigment adhere after the evaporation of the water.

Such paints can only be used for interior work, such as walls and ceiling, for coloring maps, etc. The most common paint of this kind is called Kalsomine, and is a mixture of prepared chalk, and a solution of glue in the vehicle, ultramine blue to neutralize, a faint yellow tint for white and other colors.

Naphthas and tars, both coal and wood, are used for cheap paints for protecting iron ships' bottoms.

Artists' colors are prepared very carefully, and are composed of pigments ground in a small quantity of very fine oil and put up in metallic tubes.

It is estimated that material for making pure paints imported to the United States exceeds one hundred and twenty-five million dollars, and when mixed and sold to consumers is double this amount.

JAS. McDERMOTT,
531 Seventh Street.

Lincoln Grammar School, 8th Grade.

The above writer won the prize awarded by W. P. Fuller & Co.

A PASTEL.

IN an easy chair before the fire a young girl sits reading. After a while she wearies of her book, and, leaning her head against the cushioned top of the chair, watches the play of the firelight upon the ceiling. Ere long her eyelids droop. The flickering glow is changed into the glorious sunset, the ceiling into the sky, made gorgeous by it. The walls fade away into a beautiful garden, a veritable Paradise.

In this garden, amid a profusion of blossoming flowers, she wanders, her eyes greeted at every turn with some new splendor. The pavements are of gold, not dazzling, but tipped with refulgent rays of the sun. In her walk she stops every now and then to pluck the rarest children of the earth, with leaves unfolding like a book to reveal the power of God. At one turn she spies a bower of fragrant roses, such as a young girl would love to dream in, and here and there betwixt the venerable trees silken hammocks are swung invitingly, shaded by the gracefully drooping branches.

Intoxicated with the beauty, she gazes spell-bound, while sunset gives place to more quiet dusk, and slowly, gradually the sable curtain of night is unfolded.

With a sigh she rubs her eyes, and, as if loath to leave, the quivering lids are slowly raised.

The spell is broken.

ALICE GREENBAUM.

Girls' High School, Written in Class.

Swimming.

SWIMMING is the art of keeping the body afloat and propelling it by means of the body and hands.

The swimming of man is unnatural, but as the specific gravity of the human body is very little greater than that of water, it can be floated with very little difficulty.

The art of swimming is so exceedingly useful, not only as an exercise but as a means of preserving the life, that it should be acquired by every person.

STELLA HERMANN.

There are various modes of swimming, such as floating on the back, swimming on the back head first, swimming on the chest and the side stroke.

The better place for a person to swim in, is that of salt water on account of the salt; it being so much heavier than the fresh water that I think it lends support to the body, which enables him to swim easier, and another advantage of that of being salt is on account of the saltness and bitterness, which to the swimmer is very unpleasant, and he takes good care to keep his lips tightly shut, and so does not commit the usual blunder of opening the mouth which is fatal to all swimmers, and is sure to discourage the beginner by letting water go down his throat, thus choking him.

The greater part of the above subject I have gained by my own experience, and found also that "perseverance" is the principal point in learning, as there are different things to a new beginner to overcome, such as one's first venture in the water. One naturally feels the cold, and then the fear of going to the bottom when he attempts to swim makes him watchful in regard to the second attempt, and the loss of presence of mind which comes to a person who is just learning, and which is the most dangerous of all to a swimmer.

After a bather has conquered the stroke he feels the benefits of his baths, such as the muscular development of the body and the cooling and refreshing after effects, and also confidence in oneself, which shows how easily a person may gain success with the same, not only in the act of swimming but in all branches of life.

Havard says :

> " Perseverance is a Roman virtue,
> That wins each God-like act, and plucks success
> E'en from the spear-proof crest of rugged danger."

STELLA HERMANN,
1813 Pine Street.

Denman Grammar School, 8th Grade.

That Boy.

WHO is it rushes through the house
    Hunting wildly for his jacket,
      Who is it almost drives one mad
With his continuous racket ?
      That boy !

Who is it wakes the neighborhood
With Indian whoops and dances?
Who is it marshals all his troops
And 'gainst the foe advances ?
      That boy !

Who is it slides the balustrades,
The seats of trousers tearing,
Who is it pulls poor pussy's tail,
Nor for her cries much caring ?
      That boy !

But though that boy has many faults,
He is good and noble hearted.
He is the sunshine of our lives
When by mischief he's not started.

MINNIE NEWFIELD.

Girls' High School, Written in Class.

Carriage Materials.

WE learn that there has been a great evolution in the manufacture of vehicles during the past twenty years in the United States. This has been brought about by improved machinery and the principle of division of labor applied, and by making all parts in duplicate. Large factories have sprung up in the Middle Western States, some of them employing as high as fifteen hundred mechanics. Ohio, Indiana, Michigan, West Virginia, Tennessee and North Carolina furnish at least seventy-five per cent. of the hickory, ash and poplar that go into the construction of vehicles. This system has greatly reduced the price of vehicles, and has placed them within the reach of almost any one, so that now there are vast numbers used as compared with the limited number in former years.

The spokes and rims of the finest and lightest vehicles are made from second-growth hickory trees, which grow in open spaces comparatively isolated, making the fiber of the wood extremely tenacious. Forest hickory, or large trees, are only used in the cheapest grades of vehicles.

The finest refined iron and steel are used in the construction of fine vehicles. All are highly polished by emery wheels and emery belts. The axles are made of the finest steel, case hardened, and the axle ground into the box in emery dust, making a fit as perfect as the glass cork in a bottle.

In the trimming, broadcloth, goatskins and fine hand-buffed leather are the principal materials used. The cushions and backs are stuffed with curled hair, usually obtained in South America. In the cheaper grades of vehicles, curled moss, a

CHAS. G. KUEHN.

fiber which grows on the trees in Florida and other Southern States, is used.

No branch of carriage-making contributes more to the general appearance of the carriage than that of the painter. His paints must be of the finest quality, in order to stand the exposure in all kinds of weather. The varnish used is copal, of which two kinds are required, the finest for finishing the body, and the second for finishing the gear. A well-finished carriage receives in the neighborhood of twenty-five coats of paint and varnish. Many of these coats have to be rubbed down with pumice stone so as to bring out a uniform surface when the final coat or flowing varnish is applied in a room heated at a temperature of about one hundred, and the workmen return to the factory late in the evening to turn the work over, that the varnish may not "run." There is nothing more beautiful than a highly finished carriage, and no cut or drawing can be made to do it justice.

CHAS. G. KUEHN,
612 Post Street.

Lincoln Grammar School, 7th Grade.

The above writer won the prize awarded by The Columbus Buggy Company.

Apostrophe to the Brook.

MOUNTAIN brook, with silver song
   Dashing down the hillside steep,
   What sing you as you plunge along,
And o'er the rocky ledges leap ?

To the brooklet in the valley,
Gliding through the meadows fair,
Do you echo forth a sally,
As you rush to meet her there ?

Or is your music for the flowers
On your mossy banks so green,
Bending 'neath your spraying showers,
Dashed in crystal drops so sheen ?

Well, what e'er it is you're singing,
'Tis a bright, refreshing song ;
In my heart it's ever ringing,
As you swiftly race along.

NELLIE HENSEL.

Girls' High School, Written in Class

10

Carriage Manufacture.

A CARRIAGE is a vehicle used for the transfer of human beings and merchandise. They are generally mounted on wheels, but the sledge and the litter are types of exception to this rule. They include a variety of forms, ranging from the humble wheel-barrow and rude farm cart up to the luxuriously appointed sleeping cars of railways, and the state carriages of royalty.

The use of certain kinds of carriages dates from a very remote antiquity.

The Romans were the first to use carriages as private conveyances, as the chariots of Egypt were reserved for rulers and warriors. Covered carriages were known in the begining of the 16th century, but their use was confined to ladies of the first rank.

Occasional allusion is made to the use of some kinds of vehicles in England during the Middle Ages. In "The Squyr of Low Degree," a poem of a period anterior to Chaucer, a description of a sumptuous carriage occurs. The oldest carriages in England were known as chares, cars, chariots, caroaches and whirlicotes ; but these became less fashionable when Ann, the wife of Richard II, showed the English ladies how gracefully she could ride in the side saddle. Coaches became so common in the early part of the 17th century, they were estimated to number more than 6,000 in London and its surrounding country. The prototype of the modern omnibus first commenced in the streets of Paris on the 16th of March, 1662, going at a fixed hour at a stated fare of five sous. In 1637 there were in London and Westminister fifty hackney coaches, and in 1715 they had increased to eight hundred. In about 1820 it was supplanted by the cabriole de place, now shortened to "cab," which had previously held a most important place in Paris. In 1813 there were 1,150 flying in the Parisian streets.

Mr. Harrison, the inventor, whose name attaches to the London two-wheeled vehicle to the present day, patented his cab in 1834. On this vast improvements were made, and in 1836 a company was formed for establishing hansom cabs, the same as now in use. Of coaches possessing a history, the two best known in the United Kingdom are Her Majesty's state coach and that of the Lord Mayor of London. The latter being the oldest, having been first used in 1757.

The forms of carriages now built are so numerous as almost to defy classification. The climate conditions of life and other circumstance of different countries have originated forms of carriages in each of them, some of which have come into general use, while others are seldom seen out of the countries of their origin. Among the carriages the ones most in use are the phaeton, buggy, coupé, cab, landau, victoria, dog-cart, brougham and others too numerous to mention.

MOLLIE SILVEY,

235 Eighth Street.

Franklin Grammar School, 6th Grade.

Written for the Columbus Buggy Company.

Why Stars Twinkle.

IN olden times, long years ago,
   The stars and flowers were friends, you know,
The people were corrupt and bad,
   And that is why my story's so sad.

The flowers to the stars did say,
   " We will remain awake all day
If you with your own bright light
   Will watch o'er these folks through the night."

So on this plan they both agreed,
   The flowers and stars o'er meadow and mead
Kept watch by day, and watch by night,
   But still the world didn't go aright.

Those innocent flowers thought they were to blame,
   And turned all colors from very shame ;
The poor little stars couldn't stand such a sight,
   And so kept blinking their eyes all night.

SUSIE VINCENT.

Girls' High School, Written in Class.

SARA WILSON.

BUSINESS education is one that every person should have, so as to be prepared to go forth into the world to fight the many battles with which they will come in contact.

A good education assists a person in making money, but often times people who have the knowledge are those that are the poorest.

Every parent should endeavor to give their offspring a thorough business education, so as to have them capable of taking care and supporting themselves, and if they should happen to gain riches they would be able to transact business in such a manner as to keep their property.

It is often said that a business education should be for the men and the women should do the entertaining in the parlor, but I think both should be on a level in such a case, as it is one of the most important points in our lives.

There are few parents who believe in making their daughters capable of supporting themselves. They live in hopes of their daughters marrying rich or well-to-do men, but that is not the point. If they do not know how to save, the riches will soon be gone, and then they are left in a condition very unpleasant after they have had all the luxuries of wealth.

Business comes before pleasure and to succeed in it there has to be something at the bottom of it ; everything has to have a foundation or it is a complete failure.

I have often heard of people being called shrewd business men ; it is because they have gained a good education and have put it to test ; they are careful in their transactions and do them in a systematic way.

What becomes of the widow left with property, who has only an accomplished education ? Well, the lawyers get the most of it, and by the time courts are through with it, she has nothing, poor woman, and all because she has no business knowledge and has to depend on others who take the advantage of her ignorance. If you notice carefully you will find in ninety-nine cases out of a hundred, it teaches, or ought to teach, good lessons to the parents of large families the necessity of a business education.

What a blessing it would be to this country, "The home of the true Americans," if business schools were established free of tuition. It would be long remembered and recorded among the great list of charitable deeds.

SARA WILSON,
413 Post Street.

Denman Grammar School, 8th Grade.

THE CHILDREN OF OUR BLOCK.

ALL the children of our block,
   A sorrowful thing to say,
   Consist of a most terrible stock
That ever did see day.

Their numbers I could never state,
   For they increase from day to day,
And oh ! the trouble they create
   Is enough to turn one grey.

With horns and drums they daily play,
   And make every sort of noise,
Which makes the neighbors often say
   What a blessing are those boys.

Their awful racket partly to cease,
   And us no more to assail,
Have made us threaten the police,
   But all to no avail.

M. M.

Girls' High School, Written in Class.

Coal.

COAL is a solid, inflammable, mineral substance found in the earth. It is supposed that it is formed of decayed vegetable matter, because by looking through a microscope there has been found leaves of trees, etc.

It varies in color from brown to black, according to its hardness.

Coal is divided into several classes, the most important of which is bituminous, and is used for fuel and making gases.

TOTTIE BURNESS.

Another class is called anthracite, being very hard and shiny, and burns with a very small amount of flame or smoke, but gives intense heat. It is generally used for drying hops and malt, and in furnaces where a high temperature is required. That which comes from Peru contains more than ten per cent. sulphur.

Another variety is Cannel coal and is used principally for gas; when this is cut and polished it is then commonly called jet, and is used principally for articles of jewelry. It is found in the lower part of Yorkshire, England, and in Spain.

After all the gases are expelled from the coal in the process of making gas the substance that is left is called coke, which can then be used for fuel.

The principal coal fields of the United States are found in the Appalachian region, extending through Pennsylvania, Ohio, Virginia, Eastern Kentucky, Tennessee and Alabama.

There are about twenty important collieries of Great Britain, the largest and most important being in South Wales, which is fully fifty miles long.

TOTTIE BURNESS,
520 Hill Street.

Jas. Lick Grammar School.

To Our Dead Heroes.

OUR heroes ! silent now ye rest
  Beneath the turf that covers thee,
All thy battles o'er thee are blest
By countless children from sea to sea.

Before thee monarchs oft did tremble,
Around thee now they all assemble,
And bless a nation's mighty heroes
Who for our country died to save us.

Sleep on ! brave heroes, sleep,
Sleep that sleep that knows no waking.
No more for thee the drums will beat
To call thee when the dawn is breaking.

From strangest foes and bitterest enemies
Before a mightier, thou didst not shrink, but stood to
     conquer ;
But ah ! my heroes, at last you fell
Before a Mightier Hero who rang your funeral knell.

And now adieu, my soldier's brave,
Thy county you have died to save.
And though unmarked may be thy grave
Thy name fore'er will cherished be
In this land of liberty.

L. LAVERY.

Girls' High School, Written in Class.

S WIMMING, especially in salt water, is the healthiest, simplest, prettiest and most useful exercise that one could practice. No other expands the chest, strengthens the muscles of the arms, legs, and in fact of all the body. It is said to be a remedy for diseases. Physicians in many cases recommend it to build up health and strength. It is also an accomplishment of special value in saving life in case of accident on the water. A person knowing it cannot only save his own life, but those of others.

CHAS. G. MORAGHAN.

The savages teach their children this art almost before they can walk. A rope is tied around the youngsters and let them into the water. Why should they be so early in teaching them swimming if it would not be of some great use to them ?

Some people find it difficult to learn even though it is simple. If they don't succeed in the first, second or third time, they think they'll never learn. The reason is they have no confidence in themselves. In some cases people learn themselves, that is, they may fall into the water and must swim to a safe place. I can see no reason why the people of San Francisco should not be excellent swimmers, living as we do on a peninsula almost surrounded by water.

CHAS. G. MORAGHAN,

131 Ridley Street.

Lincoln Grammar School, 8th Grade.

TO THE OCEAN.

SLEEP in thy solitude.   Oh God !
　　Into this mighty wave,
　　With naught upon the earth he trod
　　But found him here, a grave !

To thee, thou restless, moaning deep,
　　The earth must him resign ;
Alone, unknown, so still in sleep,
　　Beneath the foamy brine.

But not for aye, for this we trust,
　　So roll t'Eternity,
The body—not the soul—is dust,
　　Bathed in immortality.

Then all thy unknown treasures keep,
　　And ever be thou dumb ;
Roll on until, oh restless deep,
　　The Day of Reckoning come.

Perchance thy wave it would full-fain
　　Its pent-up feelings free,
If mortal tongue, oh mighty main,
　　Thy Maker gave to thee.

Perchance 'tis but a song to sing
　　Of Him, the Crucified,
And 'gainst the rocks His praise to ring
　　For man who lived and died.

Perchance 'tis all reproach for man
　　Thou moan by day and night,
His Maker's love and works so grand
　　That he should thus requite.

The day that He His words fulfill,
　　Oh grandest ocean, mine !
Thou shalt thy treasures give by will,
　　Not human, but Divine !

　　　　　　　ESTELLE G. FEUSIER.
Girls' High School, Written in Class.

Art.

FROM the time "Eve sewed fig leaves" and Shakespeare and Walter Scott decked their heroines' bowers with beautiful things till now needle-work tapestry, wood and ivory carvings, paintings on China and fancy statuettes have held a prominent place in all beauty-lovers' homes.

The different countries have each their peculiar style of art. As a rule the Oriental countries keep to their original characteristics, while the European styles are constantly changing and improving.

CAROLINE L. STEVENSON.

In former times the people—our great grandparents, perhaps—were content with the rude attempts at art—an old-fashioned picture, or a little colored vase, or perhaps a collection of old sea curiosities dear to some sailor's mother's heart. But now, since France, Italy and Japan have revealed to us the wonderful realities of *true* art, we are eager to have some of the foreign art as well as that produced in our own country in our homes.

Japan and China lead the world in the manufacture of tortoise shell and beaten brass articles, carvings in wood and ivory and embroidered draperies. France is noted for its bisque ornaments and fancy tissue paper devices, their bronzes have also won admirers all over the land.

In the manufacture of glassware the Chinese are not so advanced as the Europeans or Americans. A century ago their porcelain was unequaled, but now is inferior to that produced in Paris. Among the beautiful things that the Chinese make by hand are solid embroidered gowns made for the rich Chinese women, but being such handsome articles they are used for draperies by some people of other countries. In some of them the ground of the pattern is completely hidden by the embroidered figures and flowers. The unexcelled cloisonne and satenma wares of Japan are considered to be some of the finest works of art of the past and present period.

At a very early age, the Egyptians had attained great proficiency in arts and fine arts, including sculptures, paintings, weavings and works in metal. But the people at the present time in Egypt do not seem so ingenious and progressive as their ancestors.

London is not specially noted for its *fine* arts, as the people seem more interested in the common manufactures.

There are several new departures in art, viz: pyrography or burnt wood etchings and nail decorations.

CAROLINE L. STEVENSON,
2530 Sutter Street.

Hamilton Grammar School, 7th Grade.
The above writer is the winner of the prize on " Art."

That Boy!

DID you ever see that boy ?
    He was his mother's pride and joy.
    He'd fling his hat upon the hook,
Then go to the kitchen and tease the cook
For cake or pie, or p'r'aps some jam,
Then upstairs to mother, quite unlike a lamb.
Next down the street you see him run,
Eating an apple and having some fun.

He's late to dinner, as most boys are,
Gets a reprimand from his stern papa :
But a pleading word from the mother dear
Saves further confusion, and his face is clear.
Then after dinner his books come forth :
A groan as ink falls on the cloth,
A rustle of leaves till at length he's through,
Then out comes a story and a big apple, too.

When the clocks strikes ten he goes up to bed,
Pulls off his shoes and flings his head
Right in the midst of the pillows white.
And waits for his mother to kiss him goodnight.
O, who is so dear to the heart of a mother
As the naughty boy who teases his brother,
Breaks all the rules that belong to the school,
But really tries to practice " the rule."

CHRISTABEL SOBEY

Girls' High School, Written in Class.

Chocolate and Cocoa.

CHOCOLATE is made from the seeds of Theobroma Cacao reduced to a fine paste in a heated iron mortar, or by a machine, and mixed with pounded sugar and spices, as cinnamon, cloves, cardamom, vanilla, etc. The paste is then poured into moulds of white iron, in which it is allowed to cool and harden.

Chocolate is sometimes made without spices, but it is then more generally called cocoa. The paste is sometimes mixed with flour, and with Carrageen or with Iceland Moss; and for medicinal purposes with cinchona, etc. Chocolate is used as a beverage, and for this purpose is dissolved in hot water or milk. In a pure state it soon satisfies the appetite, and is very nourishing. When it contains spices it is also stimulating.

The different kinds of cocoa either consist of or are prepared from the seeds of trees of the genus Theobroma. Cocoa is very nutritious; for dietetic use, cocoa is prepared in several ways. It is made into chocolate; it is crushed into cocoa nibs, the purest state in which cocoa can be purchased in shops; or the unshelled bean is powdered in a hot mortar, or between hot rollers, which yields a paste capable of being mixed with sugar, honey, starch, etc. Sold in shops under the name of soluble cocoa, rock cocoa and common cocoa.

It is extensively cultivated in tropical America and the West Indies; also in some parts of Asia and Africa.

The fruit is somewhat like a cucumber in shape, and is six or eight inches long, yellow, and red on the side next the sun.

HENRIETTA C. LANGREHR,
1421 McAllister Street.

Golden Gate School, 4th Grade.

HENRIETTA C. LANGREHR.

The Spring.

THE snow on the mountains hath melted away,
    And softly blow zephyrs o'er field and glen,
    Jack Frost turns his back till the next winter day,
For Spring hath returned to earth once again.

Now old Mother Nature displays her best phase,
    Her bosom doth swell with motherly pride,
The stern, cold, bleak North Wind goes forth on his way,
    For this is the season of earth's fairest pride.

The cricket is chirping his queer roundelay,
    Sir Grasshopper hoppeth from grass sheath to flower
Queen Bee does her duty, to gather all day
    The sweet crystal honey from bower to bower.

The lark in her flight stops to survey the scene,
    As does also his majesty Lord Humming Bird ;
The ground round is brightened like gold-glistening sheen,
    While 'pon pasture o'er yonder are feeding the herds.

Yes, this is the picture which Spring represents,
    His reign upon earth is most beauteous of all,
He brightens all sorrows until he flies hence,
    To make way for Summer, then reigneth the Fall.

HARRIETTE SIMON.

Girl's High School, Written in Class.

Coal.

MANY thousands of years ago there were vast forests which grew in swamps covering great tracts of land. These plants grew, bloomed and died, just as our trees do to-day.

During these early ages, when the center of the earth was still exceedingly hot and the crust that had been formed was very thin, the fiery gases inside would frequently break out and upset everything on the outside.

CLEONE CUMMINGS.

Once, when such an upheaval took place, these forests were turned over with everything in them and were buried below the waters of the swamps.

On account of the heat, the pressure and certain chemical changes these trees and plants which formed the forests were gradually changed into coal.

Where the swamps were the water was deep, but during changes of the crust of the earth the bottoms of these seas were brought to the surface again and new forests grew which were in time buried like the first.

These changes took place many times in different places.

Each forest that was buried formed a layer of coal. In Kentucky the land was raised and lowered about fifteen times, and in the Joggin mines in Nova Scotia about sixty-eight times.

The outline of trees found in the coal showed that they were very large.

Coal is divided into three kinds. The anthracite or hard coal, which is found in Pennsylvania, is supposed to be the first formed, and burns with an equal heat and hardly any smoke. It was discovered in 1791, but as it needed a strong draft it could not be burned in the small open stoves which the people used at that time and it was thought worthless, but was put to good service when found that it could be used in furnaces and steam engines.

Bituminous coal is supposed to have been formed after the anthracite and is not so hard. It burns with a smoky flame and is found in the United States, but principally in England.

After the bituminous coal comes the lignite or brown coal, and was formed still later than either of the other two. It burns with a larger flame than other coals.

In the United States the coal fields cover 125,000 square miles. Anthracite coal from United States is exported to Southern Europe.

It seems strange that when millions of tons are produced yearly that every one should not be able to have it

CLEONE CUMMINGS,

1402 Bush Street.

Denman Grammar School, 8th Grade.

The Ocean.

OH, what a charm thou hast for me,
  Thou boundless ocean, grand and free !
    Thy tossing waves, that roll and roar
  And dash in foam upon the shore,
Are sweetest music to my ear ;
  Thy mighty voice I love to hear.
And when the moonlight's silvery gleam
  Lights up thy waves thou art supreme.

ELIZABETH VINCENT.

Girls' High School, Written in Class.

Why Frogs Have No Tails.

I WAS told to write in verse,
  At school this morning fair,
" Why the bullfrog has no tail ;"
  Imagine my despair !

I'm not a scientist,
  And therefore know no reason,
Unless when frogs were made
  The tail was not in season.

FLORENCE MAYNES.

Girls' High School, Written in Class.

OUT-OF-DOOR sports are practiced with great persistency of late years. That is, out-of-door sports relating to the art of athletics, comprising boxing, swimming, wrestling and performing on the trapeze, hunting, fishing and sailing a boat.

These sports bring into play the mind, for it requires skill to sail a boat, fish, hunt or practice athletic games with any show of competency, as well as the muscles, strength being a requirement which cannot be dispensed with.

CHARLES N. FISHER.

It will be noticed with no little wonderment that boys who have been raised in the country make the most honest, shrewdest and best business men, the only reason of which is that they have been brought up in a practical business way, developing their minds as well as their bodies in the toil which every country lad is subject to.

Leaving off their work, their pleasures consist in being allowed to hunt, fish and sail. During the hunt they are able, and cannot help studying the beauties of nature, wondering at the marvelous formations, and longing for books from which to learn more of the things by which they are surrounded. In this way a desire for good literature is cultivated, and the seeds of many a noble life are thus sown in the simple out-of-door pastime.

Fishing also allows wide scope for observation, and the different kinds of fish form an interesting as well as instructive subject for most people to talk about. Besides making deep study and thought necessary, this sport offers a great deal of excitement, the least nibble sending a thrill of expectancy through the whole body.

Sailing, delightful even in the roughest weather, requires

great presence of mind, good management and strength, this last being most important, for possessing the strength, the experience can be acquired afterward. This delightful outdoor sport and pastime allows one an opportunity of studying the geography and physical features of the places past which they go, thereby giving the mind something to occupy it, and extending the limited knowledge which they are capable of possessing.

Taken as a whole, the superiority of out-of-door sports over indoor sports is exhibited in so many ways that it is useless to speak of it further.

CHARLES N. FISHER,
923 McAllister Street.

South Cosmopolitan Grammar School.

A Thought.

'ER my clouded fancy an artist's day dream dawns ;
A beauteous old-time maiden for her lover mourns—
Where the violets nestle by the babbling brook,
Where an ancient oak stands in some shady nook.

The pearly teardrops glisten on her rounded cheek,
And behind her towers a lofty mountain peak,
Above whose rugged summit the golden sun doth beam,
As a Heavenly Father to the rippling stream.

EMMA PROSEK.

Girls' High School, Written in Class.

Foreign Winds.

HAT do the winds from the distant shores say,
As they pass us by on their unwearied way
To the lands where the myrrh and the myrtle grow,
Far from the regions of ice and of snow ?

They sing to us of the heroes of old,
And the hopes long banished from hearts now cold.
They whisper to us of their home far away,
Where Aeolus rules them for ever and aye.

ALICE BREESE.

Girls' High School, Written in Class.

11

Groceries.

FLORENCE RYDER.

IT was a bleak, rainy day in San Francisco. If one looked at the passers-by, each carried a number of mysterious bundles, some large, some small, all of which betoken that the day was none other than Christmas.

An old gentleman stood looking into a well-filled window of a grocery store, and as he stood two little children, a boy and a girl, came up and looked in also.

At length they began conversation: "Say, Nan, we never have any nice new clothes now, do we?" "No, not since father has been sick." "Why don't he get well?" "Now, Jamey, you know as well as I do that we haven't a cent of money, and to-day we can't have any dinner."

Here the old gentleman became very much interested, and listened to the children closely.

"We won't have any presents like we did last Christmas, will we?" continued the boy.

"No," replied the girl.

"I wish we could go home, but if we do there is nothing to eat. Oh dear, I'm so hungry!" This was too much for the old gentleman, and quickly stepping to their side he told them to "follow him." They obeyed, and when he led them into a restaurant where there was everything they could desire, they were told to order their dinner.

There was turkey, cranberry sauce, vegetables, plum pudding, etc., and when they had finished they were two happy children.

But the old gentleman was not through yet, and when they came out he led them back to the large grocery store, which looked to the eager children even more beautiful than ever before.

Up to the counter he went, spoke to the clerk in a low tone, then turned to the children and asked them what they would like in the way of groceries ; as they did not seem to know, he wisely chose them himself.

Such an abundance as he bought ! There was sugar, tea, coffee, flour, cranberries, etc. ; then across the street to the fruit store, where he bought rosy-cheeked apples, potatoes and other vegetables, and then to the market, where he bought a big turkey.

What happy children said good-bye to him as they thanked him again and again, and the old gentleman, yes, truly, he felt repaid, and would have felt doubly so could he have seen the father and mother as they opened bundle after bundle, and when on reaching the bottom of the hamper they found clothes, their cup of joy was full.

In a short time the father recovered and received work, but the old gentleman never forgot his two little friends.

FLORENCE RYDER,
1710½ Sacramento Street.
Denman Grammar School, 8th Grade.

The Mosquito Bite.

I WAS sitting on the porch
　　One pleasant summer night,
　　When an insect lighted on my nose
And gave it an awful bite.
I scratched my nose and rubbed it
　　Till I made it very red,
And when I next saw a mosquito
　　I caught and killed it dead.

MAMIE MULVIN.
Girls' High School, Written in Class.

The Brook.

LITTLE brook that glides along,
　　Sparkling in the sun's bright ray,
　　Ever singing thy merry song,
Never ceasing in thy play.

We love to hear thy pleasant sound,
　　To linger in this enchanted nook,
On thy banks we play around,
　　Yes, we love, thee, little brook.

MAMIE MULVIN.
Girls' High School, Written in Class.

GERTIE LAPIDAIRY.

The New Home Oil Heater.

HAVE you ever heard of that wonderful oil heater New Home,
That wherever 'twas sold created a boom ?
Town lots that for years you could scarce give away
Rose in price at the rate of a thousand a day ;
And sour-faced women who growled all the while
Grew rosy and fat with sweet-tempered smile ;
And husbands who often remained out quite late
Seemed at last to enjoy the marital state ;
Old topers, who hadn't been sober for years,
Joined the church and repented in sackcloth and tears ;
The doors of the jail were thrown open wide
And the guards were dismissed for no one was inside ;
Old people who suffered from rheumatic pains
Jumped and danced all about without crutches or canes ;
Farmers took up the mortgage that lay on each farm,
Merchants all had a sack of money as long as your arm ;
And what do you think caused this state of affairs,
And made humble people strut about with fine airs ?
Why ! 'twas simply an oil heater with its handle of brass
As bright as gold and as polished as glass,
Not a whit was it large nor a whit was it small,
But just the right height for the short or the tall.

In fact, 't was so nice and exactly the size,
That throughout the whole country 't was given the prize,
And Meyers & Company by its making got fame,
Till there's scarcely a man who knows not the name,
And the women agree with unanimous grace
That this man of all men is a friend to their race.
So if you'll be happy and have nice clean rooms,
Don't delay, but get one of Meyers' Oil Heaters New Home,
And next to the stars and the stripes floating free,
Universally loved will this article be.
In song and in story, in legend and rhyme,
May this name be preserved through the annals of time,
And as long as stars shine in the azaline blue
The name will be young and the Heater always new.

GERTIE LAPIDAIRE,
503 Grove Street.

John Swett Grammar School, 8th Grade.

The above writer won the prize awarded by John F. Meyers & Company.

Soliloquy to the Moon.

LUNA rose brightly ; she seemed to say, "Great sights I see as nightly through the heavens I take my course, followed by my train of twinkling stars. Great secrets are hidden in my bosom.

" Notwithstanding the music of the spheres, I still can hear the cries of woe and shouts of joy which reach my ears ; they come from the far-off Earth. But still I can sympathize with the mortals.

" Upon the deep blue sea, when all is peaceful and calm, the sailors quite forget the mercies which fall from our Maker's hand, but when by storms they are tossed they call upon Him for help and strength. Oh ! how I wish that I might use some sweet influence which would melt their stubborn hearts and turn them unto God.

" Sometimes I linger long, watching the young people at their sports and games. I often wish that I could stay to enjoy the sight, but I must hasten on to cheerfully fulfill my part in the workings of the universe.

" I wonder why we are shut in the heavens, but still I know— it is simply to remind man of his Creator, for God guides the stars in their way. I must hurry on for the king of day is fast pursuing me."

MAUDE STEVENSON.

Girls' High School, Written in Class.

Arabian Coffee.

WERE it not for the bright sunshine, the refreshing rain, the goodly care of man, where would all the beautiful coffee trees and the invigorating coffee be? They would be all gone. But since there are such things they never will be gone.

There are many kinds of coffee, but of all varieties the Arabian coffee is the best. The Arabian coffee is picked from the coffee plant of Arabia, the finest coffee producing country in the world. The culture of coffee in Arabia is as follows: When the beans or coffee berries are ripe they are gathered from the tree, and placed on native mats to dry in the sun. Until the tree is or reaches the age of three years, it does not yield any coffee. When it arrives at that age it gives a crop of about a pound of coffee beans. As the tree grows older it will give much larger crops. The culture of coffee is extending every year. Arabian coffee is superior in every respect to the Brazilian or Java coffee.

The coffee, as prepared for commerce, is roasted until a dark brownish color. After it cools it is assorted, then packed in sacks, loaded into ships and from thence to all parts of the world.

The coffee prepared for the table must first be ground into particles, then mixed with boiling water, milk and sugar, when it becomes a delicious beverage. The armies of the world use coffee to invigorate and refresh the soldiers after a long tiresome march.

KEIGE TAKEYAMA.

KEIGE TAKEYAMA,
(A Japanese boy),
403 Geary Street.

Clement Grammar School, 8th Grade.

The Place Where the Lost Things Go.

I HAD mislaid a book, and after searching a long time for it I sat down to rest and think where it could be. Suddenly, without warning, I found myself at the entrance to a large building, resting, it seemed, on clouds, and with nothing near it but clouds—clouds as far as the eye could see. A little, old lady came and admitted me to the building, and then offered to take me through it. This offer I gladly accepted, so, after telling me that it was the place where the lost things go to (I thought of my book), she led me to a large room at one side of the entrance. This was where all lost things were carried first, and as sorted out and sent to their various departments. From this room I went to what was called the "Children's Department;" here all the lost playthings were stored. Oh! that some poor, little, ragged children might be brought here. What a palace it would seem to them! There were dolls, dishes, tops, marbles, hoops, blocks, etc. (I noticed that boys' playthings were the most numerous). From here I passed into a number of rooms, one after another, all containing different things. The pin-room was particularly large and full.

The last room I visited was the largest and fullest. It was the room of "Lost Opportunities." The opportunities were put under glass cases, for they were precious, and each case was labled with the name of the loser. I passed down the room, glancing at the names; one particularly attracted my attention. I crossed to read the name. It was my own. The number of opportunities I had lost scared me and I—awoke in a shiver. I had been asleep.

There was at least one pleasing feature of the dream, I had not seen my book. It could not have been lost. But where did I put it? There was nothing to do but continue my search. Finally, I found it on the shelf where it ought to be, the last place I would have thought of looking for it.

ADELAIDE M. HOBE.

Girls' High School, Written in Class.

Education commences at the mother's knee, and every word spoken within the hearsay of little children tends towards the formation of character. —BALLOU.

Educated men are as much superior to the uneducated as are the living to the dead. —ARISTOTLE.

Outdoor Sports.

THEODORA DUTREUX.

UTDOOR sports from a hygienic point of view are essential and indispensable to the health, to say nothing of their miraculous effects upon the physical development of the body and mental development. This knowledge is noticeably being recognized by the people of the civilized world, and gaining a fast hold upon the minds of men, increasing with every decade and making its influence felt by all believers of good health.

Although the Americans were the last to recognize this fact, they are at the present age the most enthusiastic, or nearly so, of the enlightened world, the Britishers being foremost in all sporting games. We give England, therefore, the credit of having introduced into this country such games as hunting, fishing, polo, tennis, etc., which are successfully indulged in by the health-hunting and pleasure-loving element of our progressive people.

The Americans, however, boast of and claim as their own the well-known, original baseball game.

For beauty and grace, and for the general enjoyment of participants, tennis may be said to excel all other games in which the fair sex may join. When played by experts it is thoroughly scientific, and calls to action all the muscles of the body. For physical and mental development, barring certain well-known games, tennis is acknowledged as the most popular.

Another exceedingly pleasurable and excitable, as well as interesting, outdoor sport is hunting. This is declared as being both healthful, and is gaining ground in America rapidly.

THEODORA DUTREUX,
1102 Taylor Street.

Denman Grammar School, 8th Grade.

Why the Stars Twinkle.

WHEN first our Lord the un'verse made,
　　Our earth and heav'n so bright,
Before He made the dark and shade
He made the orbs of light.

And first He made a tiny thing,
　　Which e'er did brightly glisten,
And so sweet with itself did sing
　　That angels stopped to listen.

For it was proud of its light so bright,
　　Of its lovely flashing gleam,
And sang to itself with all its might,
　　" Oh show another such beam !"

But grief must come, that comes to all
　　Who fill their hearts with pride,
E'er yet God's work was fully done,
　　Our star himself did hide

Behind an angel's shelt'ring wing,
　　Which him protection lent ;
Against so bright, so grand a thing,
　　His joy was almost spent.

For when he returned *once*, to spy
　　From out his hiding place,
It dazzled so his tiny eye
　　He scarce its beams could face.

For such a lurid, glaring light
　　Did cause such constant blinking,
That if you see him *now* at night,
　　He's ever, ever winking.

MABEL N. WISE.

Girls' High School, Written in Class.

Swimming.

L. A. WOMBLE.

SWIMMING is the most useful of all athletic accomplishments, as by it human life is frequently saved, which might have been sacrificed. It is also useful in the development of muscular strength, as well as highly beneficial to the nervous system, and repairs the vital functions when falling into decline. In places near the sea or rivers to know how to swim is an indispensable accomplishment. The ancients, particularly the Greeks, held the art in such high estimation as to bestow rewards upon the most perfect swimmers.

From the little familiarity with immersion in water which the inhabitants of our towns and cities possess, a very great proportion of the American population are but little acquainted with the art of swimming, and with the mode in which they should conduct themselves where risk of drowning presents itself.

Most animals have a natural aptitude for swimming not found in man, for they will at once swim when even first thrown into the water ; but it must be noticed that the motions they then employ much more resemble their ordinary movements of progression than those made use of by men under similar circumstances.

The children of many uncivilized nations, especially in warm climates, frequent the water from an early age, and seem almost to swim by instinct. The remarkable powers of endurance, agility and strength manifested while in the water by many individuals of savage tribes are well known.

L. A. WOMBLE,
2233 Washington Street.

Pacific Heights Grammar School, 8th Grade.

"An Enchanted Garden."

I HAD wandered one evening into the redwood forests of Mariposa Valley, at some distance from the river bearing that name, when a few moments walk hid me from the open daylight and I enjoyed in all its loveliness the beauteous prospect of a contemplation of the wonders of nature.

I strolled on for a while, all the time penetrating deeper and deeper into the recesses of gloom, until having become tired I sat down. All was silent as the tomb ; not a sound could I hear, not even a twitter or chirp. Above me rose the regal redwoods, towering aloft like fabled giants with their bushy heads. Here, buried within the depths of this silent vastness, I became overpowered with a feeling of awe, which developed into a sort of terror.

As the evening advanced the gloom deepened and a breeze sprung up which crept among the treetops with a low rustling like the sullen roar of distant thunder. Again all was silent and repose save the fall of some leaf, the transient sighing of some passing wind or the hooting of the sleepless owl. The grandeur, the astonishing solemnity of this scene, cannot be expressed in language, nor can the most extravagant fancy of the imagination equal it.

Retracing my steps I soon approached the edge of the forest through which the struggling beams of the rising moon lit up the surroundings. I could now hear the rushing of the mountain river as with booming sound it rose and fell in the distance, filling the ear of night with its wild and continuous melody.

The scent-laden breeze that had risen with the queen of night seemed to precede her triumphal course with her perfumed breath. The golden luminary slowly ascended the firmament, now peacefully pursuing her course through the azure sky, now hidden beneath the banks of snowy clouds that drifted lazily toward the east.

The roar of the midnight express with the fiery glare of its headlight but momentarily broke the stillness of the night. Neither eye or the imagination need have gone further than that redwood forest to have felt the presence and existence of a supreme God, to have perceived within those gloomy arches something more than the death-like silence and grandeur.

Perfectly content with what I had witnessed I retired, feeling confident that I really had seen " An Enchanted Garden."

ALICE PLEASANT.

Girls' High School, Written in Class.

Outdoor Sports.

IDA PRECHT.

OF all outdoor sports I admire hunting and fishing the most. No other pursuits put one so in touch with nature, and once you offer Dame Nature a willing hand she will lead you to her choicest retreats, and reveal to your vision treasures the uninitiated mortal could neither perceive nor dream of.

What artificially rendered music can compare to the murmuring of the brook at your feet as it flows merrily here, silently there or turbulently over some narrow rocky places until lost in the dreamy distance ?

Rod in hand, you wander along the bank of the brook, casting your lure here and there, stepping carefully over stones and bunches of grass, and adding an occasional speckled beauty to the dozen already in your basket.

Now, for a moment you almost forget fishing, as scare ten feet away a beautiful silver gray tree-squirrel runs up the trunk of a sweeping alder, and at half that distance to your left, on a heap of dry branches, a little chip-munk stares impudently in your face. Involuntarily you move a foot and both disappear, and in the next moment you are almost startled by the whirr of a quail getting up from under your feet.

You keep on lazily moving down stream when a large trout jumps most two feet in the air. For the moment you forget everything else but that fish, and you want him badly. You clear away your line from the rod, and at second cast your flies drop softly as thistle-down right in the middle of the rings left on the surface of the water by the monarch of the pool. You scarcely begin to move your rod when there is a sudden com-

motion in the direction of your flies, involuntarily you give a
slight turn of the wrist and an electric shock runs through
your whole being as you instantly realize that you have fastened to at least a " two-pounder."

How your reel sings out sweet music : how evenly your pet
rod bends from tip to butt !

Next to fishing I consider hunting the most attractive of outdoor sports. True, it is a more laborious pastime than the
former, and less adapted for ladies.

I can shoot rabbits and larks, but I wish I were a boy, and
could climb the hills like papa, and learn to shoot quail, for
that seems the most interesting of all shooting. Yes, I wish I
were a boy, and I guess papa does, too !

IDA PRECHT,

1215 Bush Street.

Denman Grammar School.

Our School Troubles.

OF all the terrors that schoolgirls enthrall,
I think geometry's worst of 'em all,
All of us dread it, though some more or less,
Our teacher can't understand it, I'm willing to confess.

Then comes the chemistry next on the list,
Interesting as well, though oft I have missed,
My equations won't balance, my experiments fail,
And, on entering, the girls pleasant odors inhale.

Our history, although we like it, is hard,
I anxiously sit, till from off the card
I hear my name called, then I quickly arise,
And as usual fail, as you may surmise.

And last, but not least, comes our "Burke" and our myths,
Which I dearly do love, but which takes not two-fifths
Of the time that it takes me the others to do.
And now I am finished, and am glad I am through.

ALICE E. BACHMAN.

Girls' High School, Written in Class.

Statuary.

'TWAS one of those glorious eves in June,
　　When the heart of nature sings
With joy, to see the beauty chaste
　　That a summer twilight brings.

The angels had lighted the twinkling stars,
　　They danced in the dark blue sky,
And the only sound that the stillness broke
　　Was the whip-poor-will's sad cry.

I listened to nature's tempting voice
　　And my school books dropped to the floor ;
I knew it was useless to study then,
　　So I softly stole to the door.

I wandered about for an hour or more,
　　Then lay on the ground to rest,
And watched the stars as they dimpled o'er
　　The heaven's broad, blue breast.

Suddenly, swiftly, I started up
　　Half speechless with dismay,
For the stars were falling in silver showers,
　　Making it light as day.

I found I was standing in a garden fair,
  With the sweet scent of flowers filled,
And the boughs of the stately ancient trees
  Bent as the zephyr willed.

But fairest of all in that garden fair,
  I caught through the foliage green
Gleams of statues purely white,
  As fair as ever were seen.

A statue of the Venus of Milo rare
  Rose from the billowy foam
Of a sparkling miniature laughing lake
  That flowed to the blue sea-home.

Apollo stood against the trees
  With sinewy, manly grace,
A figure majestic and proudly stern
  And a beautiful triumphant face.

Some here, some there, artistically placed,
  Were statues remarkably fair,
Copied from works of Praxiteles, the Greek,
  Those famous mortals so rare.

And dim and strange as all appeared,
  Still I vaguely understood
That the statuary heightened the beauty of the scene,
  As surely naught else could.

But ere long the fair scene faded away
  And I awoke with a start of surprise,
For the stars were twinkling brightly still
  Up in the evening skies.

I was lying on the grass, quite rested now,
  But in vain I looked around
For signs of the beautiful statues
  That had strewn the carpeted ground.

'Twas only a dream, but a useful one,
  For then I learned the power
That beauty exerts on beauty
  That lasts not but for an hour.

For surely 'tis a dainty work
  Of making o'er again,
A world of marble beings
  That feel no grief nor pain.

Yet represents the living world,
And lives while death toils on,
Helping the remnants of a nation dead,
When another one is born.

MOLLIE SULLIVAN,
625 Natoma Street.

Clement Grammar School, 8th Grade.

The above writer won the prize awarded by Nathan, Dohrmann & Company.

The Storm.

THE storm is raging fiercely,
    And the wind is blowing wild,
    The waves leap up in anger
Upon the rocks so high ;
Oh, see ! how the lightning flashes,
And hear the thunder roll !
May Heaven pity those at sea
And guide them safe to land.

BLANCH ELLIOT.

Hamilton Grammar School, Written in Class.

The Mosquito.

INSECT blithe, with dainty, gauzy wing,
    Floating abroad before our anxious eye,
    You haply might deceive mankind, but ah !
He, to his sorrow, knows you have a sting.

He knows it on the peaceful summer eve
    When on piazza broad he sits at rest ;
He feels your bite ('tis thus mankind you grieve)
    And shouts, "Oh, thunder ! Catch that little pest !"

JESSIE R. WOOD.

Girls' High School, Written in Class.

Flour.

TO put the definition of flour in as few words as possible, it is merely the edible part of corn or meal, and in olden times was called flower.

Wheat-raising (flour in its crude state) is one of the principal industries of the farmers in our Golden State.

The quality of the flour depends upon the excellence of the wheat, and upon the superiority of the milling process to which it is subjected. In this work the millers exercise much skill in mixing the different varieties so as to have the flour of a uniform quality. The more the mixture reaches pure starch, the finer it is considered. After milling it passes into a long cylinder, arranged so as to revolve, and covered with a fine piece of silken cloth of a sieve-like nature. The finer meal passes through at the upper end of the cloth, and, as this varies in coarseness, the coarser meal does not pass until it reaches a like part of the cloth, and this last to pass through is classed as middlings, bran, etc.

The finest flour, however, is not the most nutritious. Graham flour, quite a coarse quality, is considered one of the most healthy cereals to be eaten.

Of late there have been several processes invented, which tend to remove the bran particle of the wheat, as well as to grind the husked grain; flour so prepared is considered more nutritive and is equally fine.

Before civilization planted its foot in America, the Indians ground their corn by rubbing it between large stones, and thus reducing it to a mealy state, no separation of the particles taking place as now.

There is wheat flour, rye flour and many other kinds, also many brands, but I shall not forget my longing to experiment with Sperry's Flour, after I had tasted the appetizing biscuit and cakes at the Mechanics' Fair a few years ago. What girl or boy does not remember the picture of the huge negro as she or he first entered the Pavilion door? The cocoanut cake in his hand looked almost good enough to eat. My first trial of this famous brand was in making muffins, and it was a decided success. They were as light as could be. When I am a woman and have a home of my own, I shall always use the best.

Those who have used other brands and have had heavy biscuits and heavy hearts, will find in using the best flour just the opposite. Both their hearts and their biscuits shall be made light, and sunshine will gleam in their homes.

ALICE POWER,
715 Lombard Street.
North Cosmopolitan Grammar School, 8th Grade.

12

Glue.

ANNA RYAN.

GLUE is made of hides, parings and other materials called Glue Stock. They are steeped for several weeks in lime water to remove the hair and blood; they are then drained and partly dried in a current of air for several days, that the lime may absorb atmospheric gases and prevent the injurious effects of the alkali upon the gelatine.

They are boiled in water until the solution is found to gelatinize firmly on cooling.

The impurities are allowed to settle, after which it is allowed to gelatinize in shallow wooden boxes, cut into slices and dried upon nets.

Glue is also made from bones by first boiling them to remove the fatty matter they contain, and then treating them with strong acid until they become quite soft; they are then washed and the acid is neutralized; they are enclosed in a covered vessel and submitted to the action of steam.

At a subsequent stage the whole mass is boiled by direct heat, and a further quantity of glue is produced.

The glue yielded by bones has a milky hue, owing to the phosphate of lime it carries with it.

Isinglass or fish glue in its raw state is the bladder of various species of fish.

A good quality of glue should have a light brownish yellow transparent appearance, and should break with a glassy fracture. It takes years of experience and practice to make good glue. Glue made in California is practically better than that made in the East.

When it is wanted for use it is broken in pieces and steeped in cold water until it softens and swells.

It is then melted over a gentle fire to a boiling point, and applied hot in a liquid state with a brush.

Glue may be kept liquid at ordinary temperature by the addition of weak nitric acid.

Under the influence of heat glue will entirely dissolve in water, forming a thin syrupy fluid.

Glue is used very extensively in nearly all the manufactories in San Francisco, and it is well to know where to get the best.

The California Glue Works of San Francisco has the best recommendation and stands peerless in its industry. It is highly recommended in the Eastern market, where large shipments are made monthly. I need not tell you where it is, as its name has become a "household word" in almost every home.

ANNA RYAN,
1134 Howard Street.

Franklin Grammar School, 6th Grade.

The above writer won the prize awarded by California Glue Works—M. Holje.

If.

WHAT a little insignificant, yet all-important word this is, and how many times we make use of it during the day. We are constantly using it in a complaining manner. How often we are heard to say, "Oh, if it were not so cold!" or "If the wind would only stop blowing!"

Many of us High School girls oftimes think, even though we do not give expression to our thoughts, if education could only be bought instead of having to drill it into our brains day in and day out, how happy and contented we would be.

Many persons' wishes are directed to other channels, some being in quest of money, while others are searching for fame, but even they are heard to complain "If it only could be obtained easier."

Many ifs go contrary to our wishes, and cause us to wear long, in fact very long, faces during the bright and sunny days when we should be all aglow with happiness.

But there is also a bright side to this monosyllabic word, and we can realize it as we look about and think of our many blessings. One of our greatest, in my estimation, depends upon that little if. If our forefathers had not fought for liberty and independence we would probably still be an English possession.

BERTHA JOHNSON.

Girls' High School, Written in Class.

Flour.

OF all human products there is none of such importance as flour. Ground from not only all of the many species of grain, but from many varieties of vegetables, it has become the most important staple of civilized humanity.

While its uses are manifold, its most ordinary use is for bread, a main article of diet, which can be found in every household of every civilized community, and in some form almost everywhere in the world. While

BERTHA GUTSTADT.

bread may be considered its main product, its use for pastry and cooking must in no wise be underestimated, as it is only limited by the ingenuity of the most expert cooks.

As to the various kinds of flour in use, it may be said with some degree of certainty that the prosperity of a people has something to do with it as well as the climate. In the poor northern countries of Europe rye flour is used to a greater extent than wheat, while among the poorer classes of Italy a flour made out of corn or maize is largely consumed. In Scotland oat meal forms a most important article of food, it being mainly used for the cooking of porridge, which has been universally famous.

As to the nutritive qualities of the various kinds of flour, it is generally conceded that wheat yields the highest percentage. Chemically considered, fine wheat flour consists of about :

Water, 13.0 parts ; Fibrin, etc., 10.5 parts ; Starch, 74.3 parts ; Fat, 0.8 parts ; Cellulose, 0.7 parts ; Mineral Matter, 0.7 parts.

Thus it is seen that all the materials requisite for animal nutrition are present in flour.

The process of milling has also much to do with the quality of flour, as through imperfect milling not only the segregation of foreign substances such as sand and dust are neglected, but important and highly nutritive parts of the grain are entirely lost to the flour. Wonderful, indeed, is the progress made in the development of milling. From the hollowed and flattened sandstones of the primitive corn-crushers to the complete steam roller mills of the present a long distance has been traversed. From the hand-feeding of a few grains at a time in the hollow of the stone, to the unceasing, tireless self-feeding of immense quantities of grain by the steam elevators, the change is almost inconceivable. It would certainly amply repay the trouble to go through some of our great mills and watch the many processes which transform wheat into flour of commerce. There are many such mills throughout the State, though in this, as in other things, there are some good but others better.

It is the pride of the San Joaquin Country to claim the best mill west of the Rocky Mountains, and it is generally conceded as a just pride, and deserves the fame it so justly earned.

BERTHA GUTSTADT,

815½ Filbert Street.

North Cosmopolitan Grammar School, 8th Grade.

The above writer won the prize awarded by the Sperry Flour Company.

Were I an Artist.

I WOULD paint the ocean's shimmer
  Under a summer sun,
I would paint the moonlight's glimmer
  After the day is done ;
I would paint the flocks returning
  Unto their folds at night,
I would paint the first faint gleaming
  Of morn's returning light.

EDITH BROWNING.

Girls' High School, Written in Class.

The Moon.

OH moon, thou queen in glory,
  Surrounded by stars so bright,
  Telling the ever-knew story
Of earth's doings ev'ry night.
Oh ! that we were like thee,
  Giving such Heavenly light,
Illum'ning the world in its beauty,
  And making all mystery light.

ALICE LOUISE MARSH.

Girls' High School, Written in Class.

Rubber Goods.

WE enter the Amazon valley in South America through the mouth of the river which has given it its name. In our sail up the stream we shall see numerous rubber trees amongst the luxuriant shrubbery whose shining green leaves glisten in the glowing tropical sun. But the product from which rubber goods are made is also found in other parts of the world.

The raw material is sometimes called caoutchouc. It exists in the milky juice of plants, growing in temperate climates, but only in tropical countries is it found in sufficient abundance to be of importance. In the milky juice it is diffused in the form of minute globules. When the juice is allowed to stand for a short time these globules separate from the watery part and form like cream on the top. It is sometimes obtained by cutting the trees down, but more commonly by making simple cuts in the trunk. In a few hours it flows out and is poured into vessels of various shapes. In a short time it thickens and becomes solid because of the evaporation of the liquid form. In order to dry it completely the practice is to expose it to a gentle heat. Its natural color is white, but it is so susceptible that it is easily and unavoidably discolored by smoke.

Some of the useful and curious properties of rubber must have been known to the natives of America before the continent was discovered. Balls of the gum of a tree are mentioned when speaking of the amusements of the natives of Hayti, in an account of the second voyage of Columbus. In a book published at Madrid in 1615, mention is made of a tree in Mexico, with a description of the mode of collecting it ; and

MARY WILLIAMS.

the author stated that the Spaniards used it on their canvas cloaks so that they would resist water. It is curious thus to note that some of the purposes to which it is used at the present time are the same as those for which it was employed nearly three centuries ago.

Its elasticity, flexibility, its insolubility in water, have been found to adapt it to a variety of uses. In the manufacture of water-proof clothing, which was the first application on a large scale, the rubber is made into a solution and spread upon the cloth.

Pure rubber is now limited only to a limited extent in the arts. The remarkable change it undergoes when mixed with sulphur was discovered by Charles Goodyear in 1843.

MARY WILLIAMS,
1719 Post Street.

Denman Grammar School, 8th Grade.

The Song the Winds are Singing.

IT WAS on a lovely summer day that I sat reading under the shade of trees in the garden. Suddenly my thoughts wandered from the story, and a pleasant sense of the nearness of music stole over me. It was the Æolian harp being played by unseen hands in the tree above my head.

I listened and I heard a soft singer. It was a mother wind singing a lullaby to her little one. Gently she told of the earthly mothers putting their babes to rest after a morning of fun. Sadly she sung of the children that had no dear one to rock them to sleep with a soothing song, and sadder still of the naughty ones that would not appreciate their mother's lullaby. Ere long the music died softly away and I knew that the mother wind had left her little one in By-lo-town.

Entranced by the melody I had just heard, I did not move for fear of breaking the spell. I heard another song, a little louder and less musical. It was the father wind just returned home after a hard day's work in the different parts of San Francisco. Spellbound, I heard him tell of the varying scenes of which he was an unobserved listener, and of the tricks he played on the people he met.

Just at this part of the song some one came up the garden path and broke the spell. I could hear the voice no more.

LIZZIE O'BRIEN.

Girls' High School, Written in Class.

Wellington Coal.

THE discovery of gold in California at Sutter's Mill in 1848 caused intense excitement everywhere.

Thousands flocked to California in quest of the yellow metal, and many wasted their lives and efforts in their anxiety for wealth. Gold being their great object, but few ever dreamed of the immense wealth that lay dormant in the wonderful coal fields of the coast—yet undiscovered. As if by magic, the population of California, as well as all of the Pacific, grew with alarming rapidity. Large cities were built in a few years, and one of the greatest demands came to be that for coal, which at this time came principally from Australia and England, as the coal of the coast was of poor quality. At about that time Mr. Richard Dunsmuir discovered coal near the present site of Wellington, British Columbia. The mine was opened in the year 1872, and the superior quality of the ore assured the mine success, and it came to be known as " Wellington " coal. The mine, controlled by a company with Mr. Dunsmuir at the head, came to be known far and wide. More land is added to the claim, until now the coal fields of this company cover nearly three thousand five hundred acres. The products of the mine have increased until at the present time the daily production averages more than fifteen hundred tons of coal. The mining of this vast amount of coal gives employment to about six hundred men. The coal is brought from the mines near Wellington, B. C., by rail to Departure bay, and from there it is shipped to San Francisco and many other ports, by means of two large steamers and several sailing vessels. A large amount of the coal mined is consumed in Victoria and other cities around Puget Sound. San Francisco receives an immense quantity daily. The balance is shipped to different cities along the coast and other ports, some even going as far as Mexico and Honolulu. "Wellington" coal is without doubt the best coal obtainable on or near the Pacific Coast. Its superiority is shown by the fact that for its merits its producers were awarded a gold medal at the Midwinter Fair, San Francisco. It has stood a test of about 22 years, and speaks for itself. This coal is used nearly altogether by the city of San Francisco in public buildings, etc., and is much preferred for family use, as good coal is one of the greatest necessities of every household, wherein this product is used. One of the chief features of " Wellington " coal is the amount of carbon it contains. As shown by Mr. Price, the assayer of San Francisco, it contains fixed carbon to the amount of 56.54 per cent., other carbonaceous matter, 34 per cent., water, 2.05, and ash, 7.41 per cent. Thus we see that the coal is made up of the properties necessary for a good coal, and has held and always will hold first place as the best coal obtainable on the Pacific Coast.

J. GILBERT RECHEL,

1003 Valencia Street.

Mission Grammar School, 8th Grade.

The Wishing Ring.

THERE was once a young peasant maiden who lived in a little village with an aged grandmother. It was a long time ago, and in a far-away country where the principal thing young girls had to do was the spinning of flax. So this maiden sat in the open doorway working at her spinning-wheel all day long, and trying to believe she could never be anything but unhappy, because she was neither rich, gifted nor beautiful.

One day as she sat there gazing discontentedly at the distaff —it was a very warm, sultry day ; the bees were humming drowsily, and everything was lazy—she became aware that something had dropped into her lap. She picked it up and examined is curiously. It was a round brass ring, and on it were written these words : "Put me on your left thumb and turn me thrice around, with your heart's desire on your tongue, and see what comes of it." She hesitated—there was something about it of the terrible black art of which she was so afraid, and in terror she let it fall upon the floor.

"If I can obtain beauty or riches only by working with the Evil One, I will not wish for them at all!" She cried out so loud that the grandmother heard her and came and woke her up with a great shake—for she had been sleeping most soundly.

Then she was well scolded for being so lazy, and she promised never again to wish for things she could not have, for the fright cured her.

BESSIE W. CRABBE.

Girls' High School, Written in Class.

School Furniture.

~~~~~~~~~~

I SOMETIMES wonder how many girls of my age have gone to school in as many different places as I have.

I think I ought to be able to write about school furniture, for I have gone to school in six different States and in several different towns in some of the States.

Of course I have had a great many kinds of teachers also, and have liked them all but one ; she was my Chicago teacher, and used very unladylike language to us. She called us dumb-heads, blockheads and idiots.

I will describe the school I attended when I was spending the summer in the country in Ohio. It was built on top of a hill by the side of a road, and had no shade trees near it, and, for fear the scholars would look at the people passing, there were no windows on the side of the house next to the road, which made it very warm and unpleasant.

The furniture consisted of a table and chair for the teacher and plain wooden benches and desks for the scholars.

There are a great many respects in which school furniture could be improved ; the backs of our chairs are very uncomfortable, and often make my back ache.

Then I think the chairs and desks should be assorted as to size ; in every room there are some small and some large children ; the small boy has to sit on his foot to raise himself high enough to write, while the large boy has to crouch down in his seat and double up his legs, as the boy in front always objects to having his neighbor's feet mingling with his.

The teachers have armchairs with cushions, and they look very comfortable.

The pencil groove on the desks should be deeper, I think, and each desk should have a foot-rest and a hook on which to hang the dumb bells.

School-rooms should have cabinets for minerals, wildflowers and other specimens, also cases where the pencils and drawing books are kept.

This is about all the furniture found in the school-rooms I have been in.

I think a fine globe would be a great help in learning geography.

HILMA JONES,
1318 Octavia Street.

Clement Grammar School, 6th Grade.

Outdoor Sports.

WHY is it the children of all nations play? They play for the pleasure in the play itself. Thus negro boys of central Africa will play some sort of game, but they have not any games that we should call good, but they make their plays by imitating monkeys or some other animal in the wild forests, and practicing in throwing spears and striking with clubs.

Indian boys play with the bow and arrow, the fishing rod and tomahawk, thus imitating their fathers.

American boys play with fine games, as baseball, football, tennis, etc., which are invented by ingenious people. These games are played by the students of America, as well as boys.

The girls of all the different nations imitate their mothers, and play mother with dolls.

The boys take their position in sport just as men take position in business.

Outdoor games are different in different climates. In summer the children of the Eastern States of this country play baseball, football or some other game. In winter, while the snow and ice are on the ground, they amuse themselves by skating on the ice and sleigh-riding and coasting on the snow.

Baseball is an outdoor game played on a diamond with bat and ball, by two teams, each having nine men. Football is played with a football by two teams, each having eleven men.

Fishing is one of the most interesting games of outdoor sports. Trout-fishing needs a great deal of skill, for trout are not so easily caught. The boy who has skill can catch more trout with a poor outfit than a man with a fine outfit, but if the boy has a fine outfit he can do much better than he can with a poor outfit.

Most of the people spend their vacation in trout-fishing.

Boys often show their activity and industry by making windmills, wagons, boats and building houses instead of playing other games.

Outdoor sports make people healthy, by their being in the sun and breathing pure air, and give people strength by developing the muscles by the exercise which accompanies all sports.

There are always two kinds of people in any of the games; the one who is always unsatisfied will spoil the fun of the game, while the other who is most always satisfied makes the game more cheerful.

Boys should be always kind, cheerful and careful during the game, so as to make the game develop character as well as muscle.

The person who is studying needs exercise to make him active, so as to help him along in studying, and that he may forget his hardship of the past.

THOMAS R. TAMURA,

(Japanese Boy.)

Clement Grammar School, 7th Grade.

The above refers to the firm of George W. Shreve.

" Our Johnny."

ALL day long through the halls and the rooms,
  Marching along with hammers and brooms,
  Oh! how my heart aches to think of that boy,
He seems to know nothing but tease and annoy.

The horns and drums they sound all day,
The cat, the dog, all form array ;
He eats whate'er comes in his reach,
Should it be hard-tack, pears or peach.

His sister's hair to the chair he ties,
And with quick steps away he hies,
The cookies they vanish, and also the cake,
For "Our Johnny" is sly, and always awake.

But now "Our Johnny" is all full grown,
And his mind with higher seeds is sown,
His thoughts to loftier things devotes,
And now he is able to cast his votes.

DAISY GETZ.

Hamilton Grammar School, 8th Grade, Written in Class.

Type.

TYPE is a small block of metal with a letter or figure in relief on one end.

The invention of movable type dates as far back as the thirteenth century. It was invented by Lawrence Coster about the year 1423. While he was cutting some names on the bark of a tree the idea came to him that he might carve the letters of the alphabet, each letter on a separate block of wood ; and then by tying them together and covering them with ink he could stamp any word in the language.

The first movable metal types were probably made in 1440 by John Gutenberg. Metal letters or types were made by hand, and the " Mazarine Bible " was printed. It was the first edition of the Scriptures ever printed by movable type.[1]

The material of which books and newspaper types are now made is an alloy known as type metal. It is composed of lead, antimony, tin, and sometimes copper and other metals. More lead is used than any other metal in the alloy; antimony is used to compensate for the softness of the lead ; tin is added to give toughness, and sometimes a little copper is added to give a still greater degree of tenacity. Very little copper is used, however, as one per cent. of it gives a perceptible reddish tint to the type metal.

The durability of type has been greatly increased by the system of copper-facing, invented and patented by Dr. L. V. Newton of New York. Through the agency of the electrotype battery a thin film of copper is deposited on the face of the type, making an efficient protection against abrasion and rapid wear.

In type manufactories all the matrices of a font are made to fit one mould. The type mould consists of two firmly screwed combinations of several pieces of steel, making right and left halves, each of which is almost a counterpart of the other. These halves are immovable in the direction which determines the depth and height of the body, but readily adjustable in the direction which determines the width of the letter. Either a *I* or a *w* can be produced with no further delay than that caused by the change of matrix.

Book and newspaper types are now made by type-casting machines. In the center of the framework of the machine is a pot of melted type-metal kept fluid by a fire underneath. The melted metal is injected into the type mould by a piston and cooled by a blast of cold air. The mould flies back and drops its type and goes back again for a new supply of metal. This machine produces from about 70 types of pica to 150 types of nonpareil a minute. But the type is not yet perfect ; a piece of metal called the jet is still attached to the foot of it ; this must be broken off and the edges smoothed on grindstones ; then, if the letter is perfect, the type is ready for the printer to use.

DAVID WAHLBERG,

407 Tenth Street.

Franklin Grammar School, 8th Grade.

Only a Minute.

ONLY a minute to get the train,
The last to leave to-day.
If we are late,what will they say ?
They'll think that we delay.
Only a minute to get to school ;
What will the teacher say ?
If we are late, we'll break the rule,
And lose credits to-day.

LOLA McFEELY.

Girls' High School, Written in Class.

Apostrophe to the Ocean.

O THOU dark and deep blue ocean,
Why rollest thy billows upon the shore,
Why keepest thou up that perpetual motion?
O, answer me ! and cease that eternal roar.

How many a tale could thy bosom unfold
Of love, war and heroes so noble and brave
That their names might forever head the list of the bold
If only thy waters would speak and cease to rave.

LETTIE ROUNTREE.

Girls' High School, Written in Class.

Pictures from Poems.

SOME of the most beautiful pictures that have ever been painted have had their inspiration in the lines of some poet. It is almost impossible for two persons to have the same conception of the poet's meaning, and thus an indefinite number of pictures may be taken from the same lines. It is very hard to paint or even tell our thoughts to others, but I will try to present to your minds the pictures which these two stanzas call up in my imagination :

> The day is cold, and dark, and dreary ;
> It rains, and the wind is never weary.
> The vine still clings to the mouldering wall,
> But at every gust the dead leaves fall,
> And the day is dark and dreary.

The main objects in this picture are the old deserted mill standing by the mill-pond and the miller's house by its side. What a scene of desolation it is ! The mill-pond is covered by a green film, and the stagnant waters ripple among the rank grass on its margin. The mill, once the scene of so much hurry and bustle, stands silent and alone. Through the half-open door can be seen some remnants of the machinery, which in the days of old filled the air with its noisy clatter. Now it is left to rust and decay in silence. The home of the miller is the most forlorn of all. The boards are weather-stained and partly fallen into decay. Its chimney had long since fallen and the dusty bricks are fallen to the floor. The door round which the happy children played has fallen in and we can see the kitchen. In the palmy days, when the kitchen was the cheeriest room in the house, the whir of the spinning-wheel resounded through the room. Now the bats and owls are the only inhabitants, and the spider spins her web undisturbed. Without, the dead honeysuckle and jasmine vines still cling to the walls, but their sweet flowers have long since ceased to bloom. The dreary rain falls upon the roof, reminding one of the pattering of the childish feet which once filled the house with gladness, now gone forever. In the distance stands a grove of oaks which once added their pleasant shade to the beauty of the landscape, but the wind now sweeps by them, twisting and bending them till they seem like tortured human beings throwing their arms above them in despair. Spread above this scene of silence and decay are the sad, leaden clouds, and it almost seems as if they were shedding tears of pity over this sad reminder of happy days gone by, never to return again.

Turn with me from this forlorn picture to its companion piece, a scene of rest and beauty.

> Full in her dreamy light the moon presides,
> Shrined in a halo, mellowing as she rides ;
> And far around the forest and the stream
> Bathe in the beauty of her emerald beam.

What a scene of peace and rest ! In the foreground flows a broad, peaceful river, while behind the snow-clad mountains rear their majestic peaks to touch the sky. Between the river and the hills vast forests stretch their impenetrable depths. Above the mountains the silvery moon sends down her beams, transforming the river into a silvery stream and the snowy peaks to crystal caps. The trees cast their deep shadows on the water, making the softly flowing waters more bright by contrast with the blackness. On the banks of the stream stands a stag drinking from the cool waters. The stag does not start at every sound, fearing danger, for the hand of man has never brought discord into the calm peace and rest of this great solitude. The calm beauty of the night is undisturbed by any discordant element. It is a scene that almost makes one wish that man need never come, with his useful arts and inventions, to cut down the beautiful trees, drive the deer from his haunts and use the beautiful river for his own pleasure and profit.

MAUDE STEWARTSON.

Girls' High School.

The Wishing Stone.

IT happened on a sunshiny morn,
　　That I at very early dawn
Was tripping lightly down the lea,
When in my haste I stopped suddenly.

What was that object so bright and shiny,
Covered with letters very tiny ?
I was quite surprised to find
Nothing but a stone of ordinary kind.

It said : "This is a wishing stone
By the fairies given, and to he alone
Who finds it shall most lucky be,
And have his wish granted speedily."

Could this be true ?　I thought once more,
And I really trembled to think it o'er.
Then I said in a loud and frightened way,
Take me to Fairyland this very day.

I scarce had uttered these magic words,
When a little humming sound I heard,
And turning around from whence it came,
A tiny object did I discern.

It was a fairy all in red,
And I bent my head to hear what he said :
"So you want to go to Fairyland ?
Well, come along and take my hand."

13

At this I laughed most heartily,
Because his hand I could scarcely see,
It was so small and in fairy proportion,
That I laughed till my face was all in distortion.

When from his belt a sword he took
And over me he it gently shook ;
Then I began to shrink and bend,
Till I was no bigger than my fairy friend.

So we ran over hill, vale and dell,
And reached Fairyland just at twelve ;
And there I beheld such a wonderful sight
That I couldn't for the world about it write.

So when I returned after a week or more,
And my former size had returned as before,
I wished that I might again go away
And visit the land of the fairies gay.

Now, if you should happen to find this stone,
You must wish to see Fairyland and that alone ;
For my visit there that I enjoyed was such
That I know *you* would enjoy it just as much.

MARGARET AMES.

Girls' High School.

Photography.

PHOTOGRAPHY originated first by deguerreotype, which was a picture on copper, silver plated ; the ambertype came next, being a positive on glass. This was perfected to a negative to be printed on paper, which had to be sensitised on a silver bath. The standard paper used was albumenized paper. Improvements followed, and dry plates were the result.

Photography has become a sport as well as a trade, and I find pleasure in it as well as work. A good photograph or view is admired by every one. If the materials used are not the best, the finest results will not be obtained.

To make a fine picture the place should be as clean as possible, and where no dust can gather. The dust is the cause of spots in the negative. Some people think that these spots are in the plates, but from observation I find it different. A nice clean gallery where dust does not constantly fly, you will find the negative perfectly free from those spots.

Retouching is the art of making some shadows plainer and making the hard lines in the face soft, and to take out freckles and wrinkles. A very quick plate is always best, as it does not give the subject time to move, and makes a finer print. A good lens is the principal thing to have ; one that will bring the subject down well and sharp, and a box that does not leak light.

The principal plates are the Seed and Cramer. There are several others, but not so extensively used. The quickest plate is the Libby dry plate, which gives a sharper print than any other. It is the nearest to the wet process.

The paper has a great deal to do in making good pictures. There are several kinds of ready-made paper, the American Aristo, the Aristotype, the Solieo and others. The albumen paper was used by every photographer before this ready-made paper was put on the market. The toneing is about the same, but the albumen required more work to silver, and to make the silver bath. It will not keep so long.

To mount the picture properly is an important fact. The paste is made of corn starch, fresh every day to be sure you have good paste. If cards too thin are used they will warp as the picture dries, so a good stiff card is the best. The burnishing is to give a nice glossy finish and to give the card a graceful appearance.

VICTOR L. DUHEM,
114 Mason Street.

Lincoln Grammar School, 6th Grade.

Glue.

IT is difficult to say what animal substances are altogether useless to the glue boiler in that branch of trade. Scraps of hides, hoof, tendons and intestines of many animals, horn, the swimming bladders of fishes, rabbit skins, old gloves, and other apparently useless refuse are capable of yielding their quota to the constituents of that jelly known as glue.

Glue proper is a mixture of "Chondrin," which signifies the product derived from young bones, and "Glutin," formed from the hides and osseous parts. A larger and better quality of glue is obtainable from the glue yielding tissues of old animals.

Experience has shown that the refuse of tanning works should, to yield the most satisfactory result, be dry and tough, free from mould and not too strongly limed. If the lime bath is too strong it deteriorates the glue yielding substances. If too weak it may not act sufficiently on the scraps to destroy adhering particles of blood and flesh.

The scraps have next to be freed of the lime, for which purpose they are exposed in drums to the action of running water. After the lime is entirely washed out the " stock " is dried in the air or a shed, after which it is ready for the next process.

Next to the hides, bones are the most highly valued materials. They are roasted, crushed in a mill, boiled by steam and placed in a lime vat from one to two weeks, until they are softened.

The next process is to boil the glue. The boilers are usually constructed with false bottoms, to prevent the direct contact of the " stock " with the bottom of the boiler, and, consequently, danger of scorching. Straw is placed on these bottoms to filtrate the product, which is drawn off by stop-cocks. Where straw is not used, the stock is suspended in the boiler by a net or bag.

The formation of glue now begins, and the materials gradually settle down and become completely submerged in this liquid glue, which is kept at a boil until it is all dissolved. From time to time a sample is placed in an egg shell and set aside to cool. If a clear jelly is obtained the boiling has lasted long enough and the liquid is drawn off. Allowing the gelatine time to settle in a separating net will usually produce a clear glue.

The next process is to mold the glue. The molds are generally of sheet iron. They are filled to the brim through large funnels with strain cloths attached to their cones. The molds are either wet or greased. When solidification is complete the boxes are inverted and the glue turned out on smooth stone. After being cut to the size desired it is placed on a net to dry. After this process it is then ready for use.

LIZZIE WALSH,

Polytechnic High School, Junior Class.   29 Albion Avenue.

Type.

'TWAS Gutenberg, of Holland famed,
   Who first made use of type,
And though the time is long between,
   His mem'ry yet is ripe.

One pleasant day in summer time
   John Gutenberg made up his mind
To take his fam'ly picnicing,
   And leave all the cares behind.

Soon Gutenberg went sailing down
   A pleasant, tranquil stream,
And stopped beneath some spreading trees
   To doze off in a dream.

He soon awoke to find his wife
   And children all at play,
And forthwith made his mind to go,
   And there no longer stay.

He hurried, too, to suit the thought,
   For soon it would be dark,
But cut before he left the tree
   His name upon its bark.

He then went home in thoughtful mood,
   You surely know the rest,
How thoughts of type came to his mind,
   And how he made a test.

Those thoughts were the beginning of
   A boon to all mankind,
For type, the thoughts of Gutenberg,
   In rank leave all behind

There's naught in man's possession that
   Can claim a higher place,
There's naught upon our earth to-day
   That did more for our race.

Let's make a supposition now,
　And then, perhaps, we'll show
What type is doing for us all
　To those who do not know.

Suppose type was not thought of yet,
　And Gutenberg unknown,
For books we'd pay *tenfold* the price,
　Or have to write our own.

What power, too, our " Daily " has
　Among the populace,
Who read its daily contents as
　They scan its printed space.

Its daily circulation is
　Enormous to send out,
And only by a printing-press
　Could it be brought about.

Our schoolbooks, too, are printed by
　These types of earthly fame,
They give us thereby knowledge true,
　Which many cannot claim.

What bother did the ancients have
　In writing out their scrolls,
What nuisance, too, it must have been
　Preserving those old rolls.

No bother shall we moderns have,
　For improved types now hold
The place once held by feathered quills
　Among our folks of old.

There's naught in man's possession that
　Can claim a higher place,
There's naught upon our earth to-day
　That did more for our race.

JOSEPH F. GALLAGHER,

6 Leroy Place.

Washington Grammar School, Graduate Class '94.

A Cocoa Seed—Autobiography.

WITHIN my downy nest I slept, nor woke
    Until the sun's fierce rays my soft shell broke,
    And with my brethren was borne away
By Christopher, the Spanish gallant and gay,
But disregarded we were laid aside
Until great Anna rose in all her pride.
This English queen our worth discerned,
And for my brothers, then, the fire burned ;
But I, preserved from this by happy fate,
Still live, the mournful story to relate.

My parent tree, robbed by the hand of man,
Has lost its fruits to fill the heated pan,
But kindly Nature gives her still some more,
And spreads the fame of chocolate from shore to shore.
The dainty sugar maidens white
Her sunburnt sons embraced with all their might,
And, into gloomy prisons cast
With sweet vanilla, wait until at last,
Obeying they the cruel man's decree,
Come forth now only one, no longer three.

From many a tree, so I am told, the seeds
Are gathered to supply the countries' needs.
For many things 'tis used—the choc'late creams
That bring success unto fond lovers' dreams
By so delighting their belov'ds, are made
From this ; unto ice cream it lends its aid ;
By frosting all the cake your thanks it wins
For cov'ring up " a multitude of sins."
To stronger drinks it bravely stands at odds,
Proclaimed by all, " A nectar fit for gods."

All honor's paid the illustrious drink
That makes men healthy and able to think.
It gives them employment, itself to prepare,
For thousands are needed to make it with care.
In ev'ry age, by ev'ry kind of man
My kinsmen have been praised. I can
Recall with pride my noble ancestry,
And think with pleasure of my family
Who spread from Asia to their native strand,
Columbia, of all the fairest land.

Yet think not that, tho' shrivelled up and brown,
In any chocolate myself shall drown.
So let me rest ; my story now is done.
Please send it to Ghirardelli and Son.

This tribute, maiden, I desire to pay
To all my kinsmen who have passed away.
The moral of it, I do hope you'll see,
"No good remains fore'er unseen." Ah, me!
Well, leave me now in peace, and nevermore
Disturb my peaceful slumbers as of yore.

MAE MELROSE,
Lowell High School, Middle Class.   1310 Broderick Street.

Glue.

GLUE is a form of gelatin, which on account of its impure condition is employed only as an adhesive medium for wood, leather, paper and like substances.

In the preparations of ordinary glue the materials used are the parings and cuttings of hydes from tanyards, the ears of oxen and sheep, the skins of rabbits, cats and other animals.

The most important material used is tanyard refuse. It is steeped for some weeks in a pit with lime water, and afterwards carefully dried and stored. The object of the lime-steeping is to remove any blood and flesh which may be attached to the skin and to form a lime soap with the fatty matter it contains.

The pieces that were stored are washed before being boiled. They are then placed in hemp nets and put into an open boiler, which has a false bottom and a tap by which liquid may be run off.

The boiler is heated by direct firing, a series of boilers being arranged in the manner best fitted to obtain the greatest possible heating effect from one fire. As the boiling proceeds, test quantities of liquid are from time to time examined, and when a sample is found on cooling to form a stiff jelly, it is ready to draw off.

Usually the first boiling occupies about eight hours, and when the liquid has been drawn off more water is added, and the boiling process repeated. In this way the gelatinous matter is only exhausted after six separate boilings, occupying about two days, the last boiling yielding a darker colored glue than the first.

The glue solution is then run into wooden troughs or coolers about six feet long by two feet wide, and one foot deep, in which it sets to a firm jelly. When set, a little water is run over its surface, and with knives of suitable form it is detached from the sides and bottom, cut into uniform slices about one inch thick, and squares of these are placed on nets stretched between upright wooded frames for drying.

MARGRET SONDERUP,
Mission Grammar School, 8th Grade.   228 Nineteenth Street.

China Painting.

TO write instructions for a beginner in *china decorating* and to say what *art goods* to use is not an easy task, but I will do my best.

To commence with, the pupil must be told a great many serious things, and these perhaps of a nature which she is rarely prepared to accept. If she can turn her hand to almost anything it will not be so hard.

There are some requisites with which the student must provide herself before she uses her *paints*. The first is to make it generally understood that she is a student and not an artist. Next remember that she is studying and not manufacturing. The third thing is that whatever she does she will do it well.

If these conditions have been accepted, whether she has talent or not, success will be hers.

We will presume that she does not know how to draw. First obtain a good *French china plate*. Select a *study*, say of wild roses or forget-me-nots. Trace the design selected on *tissue-paper* and saturate a clean piece of linen rag, with good *turpentine* and *poppy oil*. Rub the *plate* thoroughly with this mixture.

Place on the plate the *impression paper*, the black side to the plate. Over this, the design already traced on *tissue paper*.

Go over this design with a *stencil* carefully, not making the line too heavy on the plate as it will soil the *paint*.

Now remove the impression papers. The design is already for the *paint*. We will decide to paint Forget-me-nots.

From your *mineral color tubes* take a little light blue, yellow, green, brown and black, place this on a very clean *porcelain pallet*. Use only *sable brushes*.

I will say right here that all the things used for this *decoration* should be obtained from a good art store, as the best work can only be accomplished with the best *material*, and at a good store you can rely on getting the best materials.

Charge one of your *brushes* with a little of the blue paint, made thin with *turpentine* and *lavender oil*.

Paint the flowers from the center to the outer edge, leaving a small circle of white in the very center of the flower.

Try and make each petal with one stroke of brush. In the center on the white put a clot of yellow paint thinned with the *turps*. Now use the green for the leaves and shade them with a little black or brown, for the sake of variation. The stems should be shaded with a little, too, so use the paint for the stem that you have used for a leaf to which it belongs. When the paint is dry any rough edge can be erased with a sharp *knife*.

The veins on the leaves can be scratched with a *steel needle*. In reality it will be scratching the paint off.

Be very careful not to get any dust on the paint, as the least speck of dust will make a flaw on the work when it is burned in the kiln.

Any *gold* for a border that is needed. I should advise that this be done by a professional, as he knows more about *gold paint*, *wheels*, and several other *art goods* that are used for the purpose, than an amateur.

EDMUND STARK,

Clement Grammar School, 8th Grade.　　　　1019 Post Street.

A Fireside Dream.

ALL day the rain fell in torrents, the wind howled mournfully, and as I stood at the window looking into the now deserted street a feeling of sadness stole over me, and I felt that the gloomy day had imparted some of its characteristics to me. Suddenly the ruddy glow from the grate reflected on the wall, and I turned away, hoping that the cheerful fire would drive away sad thoughts.

Seated before the fire I tried to read, but my eyes would not keep open, so I gave way to the drowsy feeling and was soon in the land of dreams. Yes, in the land of dreams ; but if my dreams are ever realized how happy I should be, not only because my personal interests were gratified, but because my friends' were gratified also.

I soon found myself in Europe, having traveled there with my old companion, Maude Stewartson, and what a delightful trip it was. No, we did not travel in Pullman cars where every possible convenience is rendered. We traveled as much as possible on bicycles, in order that every place of note and many places of little importance might be visited, for Maude had become a lecturer of considerable renown and was traveling preparatory to the next series of lectures. I will not dwell on the beauties of the many places visited, but on the old friends we met as we traveled from place to place.

During our stay in Paris we attended a concert at the Conservatory of Music. Who could the young lady whose entrance was received with such enthusiasm be ? Where had I seen that smiling face ? Yes, it was—it must be—our classmate, Bertha Wadham. She, too, had gone to Europe ; there to cultivate a voice that was creating a great sensation throughout the musical world. When in our room that evening Maude came to me, her countenance beaming with smiles. What new pleasure in store, I wondered. Handing me a book she told me to read a few of the poems. Gems they certainly were, but who was the author? Looking at the title page my eyes lit on a name that I had often seen before but under such different circumstances. Whose name, indeed, but Georgie Wightman.

Leaving the city where such pleasant surprises greeted us, we journeyed on to Germany, there to meet more surprises. When in Munich we were one day greeted by a classmate, Laura Call. Our surprise was great, for we were not expecting to see any old friends so far away from home. We soon guessed her mission, and inquiring about her from the artist as soon as opportunity offered we learned that she entered a studio and her paintings had found a place in many of the galleries in Europe. While in Munich we received a letter from Edith Rembraugh, who was almost inconsolable because Grace had gone to Africa, having become a missionary. She also acquainted us with the doings of many of our friends. Eva Busch had become a teacher of English in the University of California. May Blake's name was well known in the scientific circles.

Once again in the United States we were received with open arms. Maude because of her fame as a lecturer and because she was my friend. We arrived in Washington in time to attend the Inaugural Ball. Who, I wonder, was that beautiful woman who attracted so much attention? Where had I seen that bright face, where had I heard that merry laugh? Once again I looked, and then wondered how I could have forgotten even for a moment my dear friend Ethel Kennedy.

One afternoon, when we were on our way to the theatre, I was attracted by the many glances at, and the remarks about a lawyer who was then passing into our hotel accompanied by a lady. She was a classmate of ours, so we felt privileged to speak. Yes, Eva had married a lawyer and was enjoying the renown of her famous husband.

A hand laid over my eyes, a voice telling me to come to dinner, awakened me, and I once again found myself before the bright fire.

LUCILLE O'CONNELL.

Girls' High School, Written in Class.

A Trip to the Crater of Kilauea.

WE started early in the morning from Hilo, the principal town in Hawaii, riding astride on small, balking pack-mules.

Our party consisted of six, including the native guide, who prided himself on his three English words. The road from Hilo was smooth enough for a few miles, but we soon struck the hard lava bridle path, thickly bordered with the rich tropcal foliage, consisting mostly of ferns and ti plants.

We jogged along in innocent happiness, while some tiny gray clouds gathered in the sky, and before you could say "Jack Robinson" a smart shower descended, soaking us thoroughly. The weather has a habit of surprising tourists in this delightful manner. However, the sun reappeared, dried us up, and we reached the halfway house without further interruption.

Here we lunched, and after a short rest we continued our journey.

Meanwhile the landscape had completely changed, great tree ferns loomed up, and in the branches of the trees huge birds'-nest were strongly lodged. The temperature was lower, and we hurried our animals up the last mile, making a difficult journey of thirty-one miles in nine hours.

We were so stiff that dismounting was a painful ordeal ; after accomplishing this with many groans, we limped to the hotel, called Volcano House.

The next day we rested, as that evening we visited the crater. Our mules took us to the lava bed, and leaving them, we walked over it three miles.

Arriving at the crator, we were amply rewarded for our toil. The lake was very active, and belched forth great billows of liquid fire, resembling the waves of the ocean when agitated by a mighty storm. Large boulders were tossed into the air, and, rebounding, caused an overflow of lava. It was a spectacle full of awe, and gazing on it we felt our insignificance.

Finally we tore ourselves away from the fasinating sight, and retrod the lava bed, reaching the mules in an exhausted state. We rode to the hotel, and the next day returned to Hilo, after a delightful, though fatiguing journey.

EDITH M. WALLACE,

Girls' High School, Written in Class.

That Girl of Seventeen.

THERE was nothing very remarkable about this girl of seventeen,—she possessed not entrancing beauty like the heroines of story books, neither was her wit so dazzling that philosophers

"Stood fixed in steadfast gaze."

In fact, she was an ordinary every-day girl.

Remarkable as it may seem, this girl had whims. Inspired in some unaccountable way, she turned to the classics. In about a week the knowledge she acquired on this subject was marvelous, although it must be confessed she was slightly confused at times, picturing Ulysses as gazing on the horrors of Hades, while the lovely Beatrice wandered dreamily in the land of the Lotus-eaters.

At another time this young lady determined to surprise the world by her musical talent, and purchased a violin. Who can describe the agonizing tones that greeted the ears of her martyred household ; surely,

"Such music (as 'tis said)
Before was never made."

A few months afterward Miss Seventeen determined to be a poet, and priceless manuscript consisting of lame feet, words that didn't rhyme, and other deficiences, covered tables innumerable.

Painting, French and various other branches of study were victims of this young lady's whims, yet each in turn gave place to a new fancy.

People shook their heads, maiden ladies of sixty groaned, all the world gazed on this Miss as a hopeless case, forgetting she was seventeen instead of seventy. If people would only " draw the curtain of Charity" over a girl's faults and remember they were young themselves once !

MAUDE R. KENNEDY.

Girls' High School, Written in Class.

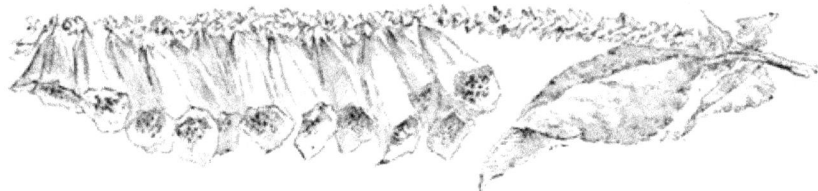

The Sewing Machine.

"THE invention all admired,
    And each how he to be the inventor missed—
    So plain it seemed once found ; which yet unfound,
Most would have thought impossible.''

So it was when the sewing machine, that great help for all
womankind, was invented. How people ever existed during
all the ages of varying fashion and gorgeous attire without a
sewing machine is a puzzling problem, for from the day that
our first parents were dismissed from the Garden of Eden the
demand for sewing has been daily increasing, and it would be
hard to tell why the great inventors among the ancient Egyptians and the more modern Saracens missed inventing so simple a thing as the sewing machine is to us.

It may be that the ancients wore simple robes because their
wives and daughters did not choose to waste time in making
garments such as ours ; but this reasoning seems faulty, when
we look at the court ladies of Elizabeth and her contemporaries
clothing themselves in garments noted for their extravagance.
We find even the men of that period beruffled, beribboned and
covered with laces. History does not tell us the number of
court seamstresses, but we can easily imagine an infinite
number of ill-fed women toiling their lives away and wishing
that something could be done to lighten their lot.

But however that may be, it was left for men of this, the
Nineteenth century, to invent the sewing machine—that mar-
vel of industry and usefulness. Little did Elias Howe, the
accredited inventor of this machine, think, as he toiled over its
mechanism in his lonely garret, what a revolution it was to
make in the labor question, for the wonderful little contrivance
has, in the course of time lightened the work of thousands of
poor women whose fingers were worn and bleeding with using
the needle from morning till night. Probably that sad tale,
'' The Song of the Shirt,'' would never have been written if
the sewing machine had been in as universal use then as it is
at this day. And little did the first inventor think that great
and various improvements were to be made upon his simple
little machine ; and perhaps he, even in his wildest fancy, did
not dream that he and many others would become millionaires
through its agency.

Suppose the sewing machine should by some mysterious

chance be suddenly taken out of our world. What confusion, what hardship would come upon us! The poor seamstress would have to work night and day upon beautiful garments for some society belle who had been thrown into a panic by the report that sewing machines no longer existed. Men would probably go back to the homespun of their grandfathers, while we women would discard our puffs and ruffles and dress as best we could. So let us now take a bit of friendly advice that reads like this : "When you find a good thing, get it."

JENNIE M. HEALD,

5 Shakespeare Street.

San Francisco Normal School.

Art.

ART did not spring into existence at an early period of man's history. The ideas of symmetry and proportion which are embodied in art decoration could not be evolved until a moderate degree of civilization had been attained.

The first af all arts was the cultivation of the soil, and the rude implements used by the first husbandman present a striking illustration of the advance of mechanical arts when compared with the agricultural machinery of the present day.

It is art that gives value to articles, and not the material of which they are made ; for instance, a flower pot made of clay costs a trifling sum, but the artist by painting, glazing, etc., transforms a very ordinary article into a beautiful and ornamental one. The more artistic the article that clay, iron or copper can be made into, the greater its value.

Bronze is one of the first materials employed by human industry ; the first used for household utensils and implements of husbandry. Later it was used for ornamental purposes, on account of being so easily worked and so well adapted to casting. It has remained from the most remote times to the present day the most effective auxiliary of sculpture. From the twelfth century down to the present day the Florentines have manufactured bronzes which for beauty of workmanship have never been excelled. Each artist had to make his own processes and do everything for himself.